1 MONTH OF
FREE
READING

at
www.ForgottenBooks.com

By purchasing this book you are eligible for one month membership to ForgottenBooks.com, giving you unlimited access to our entire collection of over 1,000,000 titles via our web site and mobile apps.

To claim your free month visit:
www.forgottenbooks.com/free961410

ISBN 978-0-260-64101-4
PIBN 10961410

Forgotten Books is a registered trademark of FB &c Ltd.
Copyright © 2018 FB &c Ltd.
FB &c Ltd, Dalton House, 60 Windsor Avenue, London, SW19 2RR.
Company number 08720141. Registered in England and Wales.

For support please visit www.forgottenbooks.com

ALUMNI MA NE

JUNE
1942

The 109th Annual Commencement Exercises in Finney Chapel, May 26

OBERLIN ALUMNI MAGAZINE

Vol. 38, No. 8

General Alumni Secretary
THOMAS E. HARRIS, '33

Editor
ALLEN M. BAILEY, '36

In This Issue

The Oberlin Alumni Magazine, June, 1942. Published monthly except in January, July, August and September. Vol. 38, No. 8. Published by the Alumni Association of Oberlin College, Inc. Subscription price $3.00 a year. Single copies, 35 cents. Entered as second-class matter October 3, 1904, at the post office, Oberlin, Ohio, under the Act of Congress of March 3, 1879.

Our apologies to Mrs. Stephen H. Millard and the Class of 1928! Mrs. Millard was through error reported to have graduated in the Class of 1929 in the May issue which told of her acceptance of the vice chairmanship of the 1942 Alumni Fund—THE EDITOR.

Photographs in this issue are by A. E. Princehorn and Andrew Stofan

My First Six Months In The Service
By Roger Garrison, '40

Roger Garrison, '40, won first prize of $50 in President Wilkins' essay contest, "My First Six Months in Military Service," conducted this past year for Oberlin alumni in the armed forces. Garrison is stationed at Camp Croft, S. C.

—EDITOR'S NOTE

M Y FIRST SIX months in the army ended in the middle of my first furlough on December 7, 1941. Naturally, the conjunction of these three happenings had some personal symbolism for me. I had spent half a year learning the profession of war and instructing others in it; I was home for the first time, a thousand miles from my post; and my country suddenly was at war. Like my country I was caught off guard—on furlough—and now there was no choice but to get on with the business: to put by the furloughs, the friendly shelter of home—to get done what had to be done.

* * * *

It was hot and crowded at the recruiting station in Boston. There were eighty of us, herded together in two ranks, saying, "I will" after the officer who read the soldier's oath: eighty civilians, self-consciously standing erect—then, presto, eighty soldiers in the Army of the United States. Somebody said, a little too loudly, "Hell, I don't feel any different." We laughed nervously, broke up into groups, perspired, felt a little trapped and hedged-in and yet, somehow, relieved that this was IT, and that it was fairly started.

That evening we arrived at Camp Devens and the Induction Center, were shepherded into a drafty barracks, given some sheets and a couple of blankets, and left to our own devices until morning. I wrote a hasty letter to my wife, tumbled onto the iron cot, and began busily to knit up the ravelled sleeve of care, undisturbed by the crap game going on in the corner.

Finds Rumors Absorbing

We were at Devens for a week, waiting for the rest of our "shipment" to come in. New uniforms (I was surprised that they fit) and a little close order drill made us feel just a bit superior to the poor rookies in civilian clothes who kept coming in every day—we'd been in almost for a week!

A recruit reception center is not much to remember. One does a little drill, stands interminably in line to be issued numberless bits of equipment, eats tremendous meals, learns to get up when the sunlight is anticipatory rather than actual, and learns to take in tremendous amounts of rumor, a commodity not peculiar to armies, but particularly absorbing to recruits. And almost every rumor was concerned with our possible destination—and when we would be shipped there.

Four hours notice was all that came before we "moved out." I got a little yellow card which said, "Your next address is Co. 'D' 33rd Inf. Tn. Bn., IRTC, Camp Croft, South Carolina. Send this to your nearest relative." My stomach did a queer turn—a thousand miles from home! Mechanically I scribbled my wife's address, dropped the card in the mailbox, and went to pack my haversack. We entrained in the late morning, and all afternoon and early evening, the slow-moving trooptrain crawled south through

New England. The wheels seemed to say, a thousand miles from home, a thousand miles from home, a thousand miles from home. We stayed for an hour in New York (my wife was five minutes away by subway, but they wouldn't even let me off the train to talk to her). I felt rotten.

* * * *

Camp Croft is a large infantry training center, a sprawling barrack-covered mushroom in the farmlands of South Carolina. The brick-red soil was baked hard and little whirlwinds of dust burst up out of nowhere as we crawled stiffly out of the train. The post band was playing noisily, and somebody began to hum Hinkey dinkey parleyvoo. It was as hot as the anteroom to hell, and the heavy uniforms itched. I could feel the sweat crawl down my back. My eyes burned, the pack was heavy and had lumps in it. Damn the dust, damn the bloody army, damn the noisy band . . . damn. We began to march down the unpaved road in ragged columns of two, glad to be out of the train, glad to be moving anywhere, glad to be doing *something*.

Assigned Corner Bed

We stood for two interminable hours in the middle of the battalion area while officers read endless lists of names, marched off small groups to barracks, and then came back to read off more names. Then our turn came, and we were marched into a clean, well-constructed barracks, and given beds in alphabetical order. I was lucky, for my name came out on the list just as the sergeant came to a corner bed. Two windows! That meant more air on the hot summer nights. It was a little piece of luck, but it made the whole day seem better. How strange that I should have a naive delight at such a simple thing! I grinned to myself: from the solemn halls of Harvard to delight at a corner bed! It was funny—and maybe refreshingly symbolic, too.

Later in the afternoon we had a chance to take a shower—and what a blessing the coolness was! It may seem stupid, but the very act of taking a shower was to become almost a ritual with us last summer; for sheer animal relief it had no equal, because we found the Carolina heat almost malignantly potent. It took us most of the summer to get used to it.

The first week was a constant round of lectures on whom to salute, what to wear and how to wear it, what was expected of us as soldiers, the Articles of War, the perils of venereal disease, and how to clean a rifle. We got shot in the arm until we crawled with anti-something microbes; we were photographed, tagged, and numbered; we collected great amounts of uniforms, cartridge belts, gas-masks, entrenching tools, a rifle, and bayonet—in short, all the equipment necessary to make of us the Compleat Soldier. We learned intimately the uses of a wet mop, of the perverseness of a stiff-bristled "GI" brush, and of the astonishing rapidity with which a barracks floor could get dirty.

We began to know our fellow soldiers and to learn, perhaps more surely than we had thought, that it "takes all kinds to make a world." In the strict equality of army living we saw a chance to make anything we chose of ourselves, solely upon what we had in us as men. With this before us, we began our training in the profession of arms.

* * * *

It was hot in the sun—105 degrees the thermometer said—and the sergeant's voice was hoarse from shouting. "On guard!" Fifty bayonets sprang forward, gleaming a little in the hot light. "Long thrust!" The bayonets jumped out and knifed at the burlap dummies before us. "Rest!" We dropped the rifle butts gratefully to the ground. I was soaked with perspiration, and my hands slipped on the smooth walnut of the rifle stock. My legs quivered with fatigue. There was a thrill in this bayonet work, though—a queer, atavistic, fighting excitement which quickened the blood and forced the lips involuntarily to tighten back from the teeth. It was a little like fencing at college; the lunge, the graceful cut of the long blade through the air, the eager searching of the point for an opponent's weakness. It was not hard to see oneself doing this in battle, lost in the tearing excitement, caught up by the nerve-wracking noise, becoming a fighting animal.

The heat was really an active enemy to us during that bayonet work. The last two days when we ran the bayonet course for record time, the temperature was a fantastic 112, and the sun was a baleful, shimmering, molten disc in the sky. We ate salt tablets, wiped the stinging sweat from our eyes, and wished that our canteens held a gallon instead of a mere quart. At noon, when we went in from the field for chow, some fellows would stand under the shower, clothes and all, with silly smiles of relief on their faces. It was not the easiest week I have ever spent, but the alternative was to toughen up or drop out . . . We got tough.

At Home With Rifle

In early August, still with the heat intense, we made the long marches out to the rifle range in the very early morning when the darkened sky had just begun to pale and lighten in the east. I liked the feeling of marching as a part of the long column of men winding along the road in the warm darkness. The smell of ripe peaches from the orchards, the flat dryness of the dust stirred by marching feet, the faint creak of rifle straps, the throaty roar of a passing truck—these things became part of a pattern which I felt rather than consciously realized. The pattern was cut away from life as we had known it only short weeks before; now it was more spare, linked with the inexorable needs of working, eating, sleeping . . . and I found it somehow deeply satisfying and real.

I liked the rifle work, too. The rugged, dependable '03 rifle, is a man's gun, amazingly accurate and easy to shoot—"that damned piece of iron," said the sergeant affectionately, "will hit where she's pointed."

It was deafening work to lie on the firing line, with a hundred rifles going at once, but most of us really enjoyed ourselves. Maybe our liking for the rifle is an inherited one, coming to us legitimately from our forebears who made this broad land a home and a way of life with a rifle and an axe.

The M-1 (Garand) is the infantry's new standard rifle, and it's a sweet weapon. My first acquaintance with it was in field firing, that is, simulated combat exercise. My squad, assembled in a fringe of woods, was to deploy from the woods, across a road, and over a small hill. We were told that silhouette targets would pop up several hundred yards away, and we were to "neutralize" them by rifle fire. In other words, here was enemy, and we were expected to kill the enemy as rapidly and as completely as possible.

Armed with the M-1's, we moved from the woods in a line of skirmishers, and advanced by short rushes through long grass, across the road, and up the hill. Since I was squad leader, it was my duty to call the proper range and to direct the firing of the squad. As I squirmed to the crest of the hill, the first targets popped up four hundred yards down the ravine and slightly to the left. "Range 400! Left front! Commence . . . FIRING!" Puffs of dust sprouted from the

khaki mounds in the grass as the squad engaged the targets. I twirled my elevation knob on the sight, caught a dim silhouette in the peep, and squeezed the trigger. The rifle kicked a little, and I was ready to fire again. In twelve seconds the targets had disappeared, all hit. I found that I had fired seven rounds. With the old rifle, dependable as it is, we could have fired two, or at the most three accurate shots apiece. Someday, perhaps soon, our very lives might depend upon the difference.

All through the long and busy summer we were on the ranges, learning about and firing all of the infantry weapons. I liked the machine gun best of all, I think; it was amazing how many bullets could be so accurately sent their way in so short a time. The mortar was, next to the machine gun, my "favorite" weapon.

The sixty-mortar, as we call it, is, with its bigger brother, the 81mm mortar, the infantry's portable light artillery. I remember, we fired it on a clear, windless day, and we had plenty of ammunition. The mortar was emplaced in a small gully, and from my position as observer I could see the faint white outline of our field targets: they were about nine hundred yards away. I called out the range data to the gunner who was crouched beside his weapon: "nine-five-oh, zero, one round." The assistant gunner pulled the pin from the shell, dropped it down the mortar. There was a noise like a firecracker in a manhole, and we could follow the shell with our eyes as it rose in a long arc toward the target. Interminable seconds later, a heavy burst mushroomed about a hundred yards beyond the target and slightly to the left. Watching the burst in graduated fieldglasses, my next order corrected the range and deflection: "Nine-oh-oh, thirty right, one round." The gunner twirled his sight knobs, set the mortar; another shell was dropped into the tube. This time we got a near-miss—about ten yards off— good enough to do tremendous damage. "Fire five!" In rapid succession the shells dropped into the tube and popped out again; all of them were in the air before the first burst came. They all hit within ten yards of the target, the third one demolishing half of the white frame. These five shells would have made a shambles of any enemy gun position. We were highly pleased; eight weeks before, none of us had ever seen a mortar, yet now we had emplaced, aimed, and fired the weapon with deadly effect within four minutes. A highly trained mortar crew can put up its gun and have the first shell in the air within fifty seconds. We were learning, by doing ourselves, the real meaning of "blitzkrieg."

* * * *

The last six weeks of our training was in tactics. In learning how to use our weapons we had learned, individually, how to employ "firepower." Now, in squads, platoons, companies, and occasionally battalions, we were learning the complicated skills of maneuver and deployment—how to "git thar fustest with the mostest."

Cleans Out Enemy

It was hard, in the early, lazy, sunny days of autumn to realize the urgent necessity of our training. We could "simulate" an enemy, but the feeling that we were playing an oversized game of cops 'n robbers was very much present. I remember one afternoon my squad was assigned the job of cleaning up an enemy entrenchment which was about a thousand yards away in the edge of a woods. We spread out, sending forward a couple of scouts, and began to crawl laboriously through the dusty grass to our objective. Suddenly the scouts signalled violently that we were "under fire," and dropped on their bellies out of sight in the grass. I crawled up to them, and then motioned the squad forward. Following every friendly bulge in the ground and moving behind each small bush, we moved on the flank of the enemy woods. About two hundred yards away, we "opened fire, and I could hear the bolts clicking and triggers snapping as my men began to lay down their fire. I sent the scouts, and two other men, down a ditch and further over on the flank to try to get close enough, while we covered them with our fire, to lob grenades at the enemy. It was a fairly successful maneuver. The umpire ruled two casualties in my forces—two of the fellows had failed to keep their tails down, he said—but he ruled, also, that the enemy was "neutralized." My casualties laughed a little nervously, we lit cigarettes, and sprawled out in the shade of the trees. One of the boys began to talk about his girl. The rest of us dozed a little. The trees rustled a little in the hot breeze. Real war, I thought, was an illusion, far away over the horizon; but in my inner mind, I knew it was coming—far in the distance there were rumblings of thunder and the faint breath of coming storm.

One night about a week later, we had a night problem. Two companies were "enemy," and my company, with the fourth company of the battalion, was to be an attack force attempting to penetrate fixed enemy positions. My squad was one of four to be chosen for the duty of combat scouting and reconnaissance; we were to penetrate enemy lines and, if possible, bring back prisoners for questioning.

Patrol Bags Officer

It was pitch dark, unrelieved by the faint starlight, as we began our cautious movement toward the enemy lines. We could not even see one another, and kept contact by whispers and touch. We knew that the enemy had outposts about fifteen hundred yards to the north of our positions, but we were not exactly sure of their exact placement or their strength. After we had gone several hundred yards, some of it on our stomachs, we were frozen by a voice which cracked out of the dark woods ahead of us. "Halt! Who's there?" We didn't move, scarcely breathing, and from the thrashing noises coming from the trees, we knew that whoever had called out was coming to investigate. Incautiously, the "voice" came out into the open, his rifle cradled in his arm, and repeated, "Halt! Who's there?" We literally rose up and smothered him, jerking his rifle from his grasp and getting our hands on his mouth before he could say another word. I sent him back to our own lines under guard, and the four of us that were left went on to see if we could capture more game.

Over to the right, quite a distance away, another sentry called out, asking for the password—must have been one of their own patrols, for we heard the word "Yankee" spoken several times in a raucous stage-whisper that carried far in the quiet darkness. Our own password was "Victory," and we were elated to have obtained the enemy pass with so little difficulty. I sent another man back to report to the commander.

As we went further into the woods, a figure passed us, walking boldly upright, apparently feeling that he was safe. We reasoned by this that we were well within the enemy lines. The figure stopped only a few yards beyond the tree stump behind which I was crouching; he looked at his watch, foolishly lighting a match. I sneaked up behind him, jabbed my rifle into the small of his back, and whispered, "You will turn around. You will make no noise." I felt a bit like Billy the Kid, and almost snickered at the thought right there in the darkness. We had bagged an officer—a lieutenant. He was very angry, and kept whispering to us heatedly that "we'd find ourselves in trouble because of this." We only prodded him with our rifles and concentrated our efforts in getting back to our own lines.

This was my first patrol. On the second trip out, my

patrol was ignominiously captured by one man, who was elated to have captured a whole patrol in one swoop. We spent the rest of the night in the enemy's "concentration camp," cussing ourselves for being stupid, but somewhat consoled that we had bagged an officer first.

* * * *

One of my best memories is of the twenty mile night march that our battalion took late in the summer. Strict discipline was to be observed, and we were told that the march was to be made in the same manner as it might be made under combat conditions.

It was just beginning to get dark when we started out—a long column of twos, the men marching at ease, the lines of rifle-muzzles swaying rhythmically, the trucks and command car trailing us in the rear—and the heat of the day was still oppressive and enveloping. Slowly, like a long scaly-backed serpent, we moved out into country roads, the soft dust swirling about our feet and covering our leggings. The sunset splashed great purple banners overhead and glowed gold from the windows of a deserted house. Darkness seeped into the trees and flowed imperceptibly over the hills. Watching the road as we marched, it began to stand out like a tangled white thread on the dark blanket of the fields and woods. The whole world narrowed down to the road, the moving feet, the breathing, moving quiet of the long column lost in the darkness up ahead. The thought scurried across my mind: the sun set at our backs, and now we marched toward where the dawn would lift our eyes. It was dark, now, deep darkness; but the road was clear, our feet were sure upon it.

The pack was getting a little heavier, the rifle strap irked a bit. I hitched my shoulders, gripped the rifle a little more firmly, and put one foot after the other.

* * * *

After fourteen weeks of training, my group was finished, and we waited around now for shipping orders. I had been made a corporal several weeks before, and I knew that I was to stay on as an instructor for a new group which was due in a week or so. It was a little sad to see these new friends—by now we were old comrades— go out to every part of the country. They were soldiers now—they even talked and thought like soldiers, though barely three months before they had been nervous boys in civilian clothes, reporting for induction. I wondered what long months and maybe years of trouble lay ahead of us before we would be "outside" again. Still, there was much consolation—yes, satisfaction—that we were of the right age to do a job that needed doing. Most of the men, though inarticulate even to themselves about it, felt a secret pride in being soldiers: the long weeks of training, the bodily discipline, the physical well-being—all these had done things to the mind as well, and for the most part, we were better men because of it. We came to look for merit in a man, as a man, regardless of his former status and privileges, and we felt ourselves being measured by the same inflexible standard. The pride of being a man in a man's world is not false or vain; it becomes one of the sources of inner dignity that makes all trials easier to bear with grace and fortitude. The time would come, many of us knew, when we would have need of that pride and dignity and when we would acquit ourselves better because of it.

. . . . .

It was quite marvellous to be a training corporal. When our new rookies came into camp, full of questions, a little resentful and truculent about the new authorities over them, yet eager to learn as much as they could about their new trade, I knew just how they felt. The army hadn't yet become so familiar to me that I was bored with their curiosity or annoyed with their ignorance of army ways. Here, I felt,

Continued on page 5

HOW FRESH THE SPLINTERS

Commencement Address by President Wilkins

If I take this dry twig and break it, and if it behaves as a good dry twig ought to behave, the splintered ends will fit together again so perfectly that one could hardly tell, by sight alone, that the twig had ever been broken.

I can remember doing this same thing, sometimes, as a boy in the woods. But I should probably have forgotten it long ago, were it not for the fact that in college I discovered that another boy must have liked to do the same thing. That other boy was Robert Browning. In a poem entitled "In Three Days," a poem whose theme is meeting after separation, he wrote these lines:

> Feel, where thy life broke off from mine,
> How fresh the splinters keep and fine,—
> Only a touch and we combine!

May this be true of us, now that you are going away— may this be true of you and Oberlin!

The most natural type of returning, I suppose, is afforded by class reunions at Commencement time. The presence of so many alumni here today, even under war conditions, is ample proof that there are those to whom this type of returning means a great deal. To me personally, as a member of my own college class, each succeeding class reunion has meant more than any previous one. So it is out of a very happy personal experience that I wish you many happy class reunions.

Return While College Is In Session

I wish you also many individual returns, at times when the college is in normal session. You will miss your classmates; but if you come back in the next year or two you will find many undergraduate friends, and you will always find older friends who will be glad to see you. My own student hour is also alumni hour—and if you can't come in at that time you can come at any other time. If you do come back while college is in session, stay for more than a single day, if you can, and enter again into the normal life of the college just as much as you can. That would mean revisiting some classes, perhaps even getting up a day's assignment, and doing some work in the Library. It might even mean writing a term paper—some of you have done that in a very short space of time before now. But you wouldn't have to take any blue books. Come to Chapel, watch some kind of athletic contest, play golf or tennis, go to a Forum lecture, or a Dramatic Association play, or an Artist Recital, or "Students," or some other concert. Visit the Art Museum, read the current Review, buy something in the familiar shops, and do at least a little strolling under the old—and new—elm trees.

I suggest also the possibility of planned group returns: the possibility that three or four of you should plan to meet here for a day or two, and do these things together. That hasn't been tried very often: it should work out very well.

But reunion with Oberlin does not necessarily involve a physical return. It may mean keeping consciously in touch with Oberlin wherever you are. Not necessarily by long distance telephone—though I wrote one member of last year's class a few days ago that he could reverse the charges or cable me collect from anywhere on earth.

It is in particular our very strong desire to keep in touch with all of you who enter military service. If you will do your part by letting us know your changing addresses—just a note or a postcard addressed either to me or to the Secretary of Oberlin College is enough—we shall do everything we can to keep in touch with you.

The staff of the Review authorizes me to say that, sharing equally with the College, they will send the Review regularly and without cost to any Oberlin man in service who asks for it; the Alumni Association authorizes me to say that they will send the Alumni Magazine regularly and without cost to any Oberlin man in service who asks for it; each of you will hear from me, when we first learn of your entrance into the service, and I shall gladly answer any letters that you may write me; the faculty in general will be glad to do likewise; if you have time to take an extension course, we will arrange that for you without cost; if any one of you, in the service, wants a book, and will write me just saying "Please send me a book," you will get one— though it may be paper-bound; and you will get occasional cards and other Oberlin material anyhow. These things we have been doing with those already in the service, and shall gladly continue with you. And I am glad now to make you one new offer. If any one of you wants to write to any other man in the service, but doesn't know his address, all you have to do is to write him in my care, and your letter will be forwarded to him—unopened. If a letter is censored when you get it, the censorship will not be the work of anyone in Oberlin. And when you have a furlough, come back to Oberlin if you can, and write your name, following the names of men you will know, in our Furlough Book.

Will Forward Alumni Letters

But our desire to keep in touch with you is by no means limited to those of you who will be in military service. It includes all the rest of you. In the nature of things we can hardly extend all of the same offers to all of you. I wish we could; for the relationships established already by the maintenance of these offers have taught us a good deal. But two of these offers do hold good for you all. The first is that I shall be glad to receive and to answer any letter that any one of you may write me, and that the faculty in general will be glad to do likewise; and the second, which I make with the authorization of the Alumni Association, is an offer which from now on applies to all Oberlin alumni— that if any alumnus or alumna wants to write to any other member of the alumni body but does not know his or her address, the letter may be addressed in care of the Oberlin Alumni Association, and will be duly forwarded.

Reunion with Oberlin, in these and other similar ways, may mean even more, I hope, to this present class of 1942 than it has meant to any other class in our long history. It may be a long time before any other great company of students spends four years together here.

But reunion with Oberlin may well mean more than the sum total of all possible reunions by visit and by correspondence. For it may mean constant reunion, unlimited by distance or by lapse of time, with that which is, in reality, Oberlin.

Many of you, indeed, will be engaged in enterprises which will in some sense continue or resume the interests and activities and convictions of your student days—enterprises in which you may gain strength from the memory of some experience here, and from the certainty that the College is providing similiar experience for those who follow in your places. I might mention many such enterprises; I will mention only one: the reestablishment, or rather the first true establishment, of peace. With all the tragedy of this war, I would not have it end—for the sake of the vast ultimate majority of all mankind I would not have it end, for your own sakes I would not have it end—until the victory of freedom is assured. But when that victory comes we shall face what may be in some ways a still harder, though less tragic, struggle: the struggle to build new and sure foundations for the world's common civilization. No one of you can say that the life of Oberlin, in your day, has been without elements that have tended in some measure to qualify you for that struggle. It is my dearest hope that I may be working with you when the world is free for reconstruction.

But for success in that struggle, and for success in any other enterprise of high human significance, we shall need that which is most essentially Oberlin. There would be differences among us in our definition of that essence; and to some extent those differences will always remain, though the years will tend to bring convergence. But for myself, having in mind alike the actual record of the long past, the deep intention of these recent years, and a well-justified hope for the future, I should say that the essence of Oberlin lies in the belief that for the good life, whether for the individual or for the community or for the nation or for humanity, two qualities are necessary, and are necessary in combination. These two qualities, both perfectly simple, perfectly elemental, are intelligence and unselfishness. To each of these qualities you may add—as I do in my own thought—whatever defining adjectives seem to you most important: but these two qualities are in themselves the continuing nouns, the continuing substances.

I believe it fair to say that these two qualities have grown, in most of you, during your four years in Oberlin, and that they are so rooted and nurtured in you now as to give promise of continuing growth.

Must Combine Two Qualities

But I also believe—and this would be true for any graduating class—that you have hardly begun to learn that for the attainment of real advance in individual life or in societal life, the two qualities must be combined, each constantly purifying the other, each constantly reenforcing the other. Of this, I think, only life itself can finally convince you. But human history is strewn with the havoc wrought by intelligence unaccompanied by unselfishness, and with the disastrous futilities wrought by unselfishness unaccompanied by intelligence.

The maintenance of mere intelligence is hard enough—it is so easy to relapse into intellectual inertia or oversimplification or prejudice, so easy to think that one's own intelligence needs no schooling, so easy to assume, without evidence, that what one inclines to believe is really true, so easy to confine one's thought to that which is immediate, so easy to turn aside from the austere paths of truth, from the exhausting unfinished trails of discovery. The maintenance of mere unselfishness is hard enough—it is so easy to let it remain negative, so easy to let it evaporate into sentimentalism, so easy to mistake one's own excitement for unselfishness, so easy to lose unselfishness when the world cold-shoulders or maltreats one, so easy to rest content in small success.

It is harder still to combine the two qualities in one interacting creativity. Yet it is only through this synthesis—unselfishness constantly setting goals for intelligence, intelligence constantly molding unselfishness into efficiency—it is only through the achievement and the practice of this synthesis that you as individuals and the world as a whole can approach the fullness of life that lies potentially before you. It will take unselfishness to make the world safe for intelligence; and it will take intelligence to make the world safe for unselfishness.

And I believe that as you come more and more fully into the realization and acceptance of the necessity of this synthesis, you will increasingly be conscious of reunion with Oberlin.

Feel, where thy life broke off from mine,
How fresh the splinters keep and fine,—
Only a touch and we combine!

MY FIRST SIX MONTHS (Contd.)

was the raw material from which could be made good soldiers or bad—and how good or bad depended to a great extent upon how efficient a teacher I was. The corporal, though only a step above a private in the hierarchy of the army, is still in a position to be both close to the men and yet in some authority over them; if he is a good soldier himself, the chances are that the men under him will be good soldiers also. I felt my responsibility very much, and threw myself completely into the job of teacher. The enthusiasm repaid itself many times over in the satisfaction of seeing the men learn quickly all the complicated arts of war. To teach them well, I thought, may mean life or death to them; and so, thinking that I could not stint of myself—that would have been criminal.

I found the rewards of a teacher to be those of an artist, almost: the raw material, shaped and guided, became that which was aimed at and designed. I felt, to be a little facetious, like a military Pygmalion. I took great pride that the men I had trained were as good on the rifle range as any others in the company; I felt an almost fatherly glow for them when they executed a particularly good tactical problem. Perhaps this kind of speculation is a bit absurd, but it was part and parcel of my early months as an instructor, and I must be true to my picture.

* * * *

Looking back on those first six months in the army, I find the memory of them good. The first weeks at Croft—how brutally hot it was, and how hard the punishing physical labor in the sun! Even now, in the mild Carolina winter, I can feel the prickling sweat on my back and the slippery rifle stock in my hands. I remember the blessed relief of the shower-bath at the end of a day, and the comfort of stretching one's back on his cot in the early evening. I remember the warm mornings at five when, out of the darkness, the reveille report was made—and the feeling of a thousand men in ranks, the whole dark mass breathing softly, voices of the sergeants: "Sir 'D' Comp'ny all present 'n 'counted FOR!" I remember, too, the short minutes that we had at the end of every hour when we could lie in the grass, or in the warm pine needles of the woods, and look up into the blue sky through the trees.

There are things that grow in a man, some kinds of knowledge that are drawn into him as the dry earth drinks thirstily of rain: this good land! This is my heritage, for this I would fight and struggle and die. On this land, men have had a dream of freedom . . . and for that dream, men will always fight.

COMMENCEMENT NEWS

Lacking many of the activities of normal years, the 109th annual Commencement Week and the first during World War II, held May 23-26, nevertheless attracted 450 Alumni who registered at the headquarters in Peters Hall.

The shortening of the school year with the earlier date for Commencement, the lack of housing facilities, transportation difficulties, and other factors contributed to the lowered attendance.

The Commencement program though abbreviated, combined for the first time in years the graduation of degree candidates in not only the College and the Conservatory, but the Graduate School of Theology. Previously the Graduate School of Theology has held an earlier Commencement. The Commencement probably was the last large scale one for the duration as students now will receive degrees three times a year at the conclusion of each term.

Some of the high points of the Commencement Week are carried below, others such as the Commencement Address, the honorary degrees, class reunions, and award of the Alumni Medal, are noted elsewhere in the magazine.

Reverend Norman Peale
Gives Baccalaureate Sermon

The Reverend Norman Vincent Peale, pastor of the Marble Collegiate Reformed Church of New York City delivered the Baccalaureate Sermon on the subject "The Amazing Power of Spiritual Thinking." He said the only way to a better social order and to international peace was through positive thinking, a changed mentality, a new premise or approach "all of which depends upon a rebirth of the religious spirit, upon a new faith in the supremacy of Christ's ideals."

He spoke of religion as a significant aid in coping with the strains and stresses thrust upon people today. "The great American disease today is tension, nervousness, rigidity," he said, as he told of how young people today in making war-time adjustments need the ministry of religion conceived in terms of a religio-psychiatric approach to the problem.

Dr. Peale believes that the basic answer to our national and international problem is a resurgence of spiritually-minded thinking by an ever increasing number of people who have learned to use their minds rationally, according to the mind of Christ.

"There can be little sound or constructive thinking out of problems when the citizenship is agitated by constantly stimulated emotional responses. The hardest kind of thinking is required to solve the problems of our times, but before we can become expert in that sort of thinking we as a people must have peace in the inner life. It is one of religion's great functions properly to coordinate and discipline the emotions."

Alumni Officers for 1942-43
Elected; Still Lack President

With the exception of the new president, the officers of the Alumni Association were elected at the annual meeting, May 24. The nominating committee's candidate for president was unable to accept the nomination and the committee is now giving the matter further consideration.

The other officers are first vice president, Mrs. Marian Warren Moore, '21; second vice president, Fred S. McConnell, '99; secretary, Mrs. Alice Lockwood Andrews, '21; treasurer, Grover Hull, '08; and member-at-large, Benjamin F. McMahon, '05.

Counsellors-at-large named were John Jameson, '18; James H. Griswold, '98; Carroll K. Shaw, '28; Mrs. Birger Engstrom, '18; and S. Lyle Hudson, '28.

The proposed amendments to the Regulations of the Alumni Association regarding the terms of office of the officers, and the moving of the semi-annual meeting to Fall Homecoming Day, of which the full texts were given in the May issue, were both passed.

Speakers at the meeting were President Wilkins, who reviewed the past year and commented on the war-time College program; and, Thomas E. Harris, the new alumni secretary. President Peirce presided and made the award of the Alumni Medal to George M. Jones, '94. Full details on the award are on page 14.

Dr. Hu Shih Speakes
At Alumni Luncheon

Predicting that the alumni association may turn out to be "the cornerstone upon which the freedom and the future of academic life may depend," Dr. Hu Shih, Chinese Ambassador to the United States and Oberlin's "youngest graduate," spoke to 600 alumni, parents and faculty at the Alumni Luncheon, May 26.

Dr Hu contrasted the long life of colleges and universities in the United States and Europe with those in China where today not one is more than 50 years old. Chinese Universities, he pointed out, existed in the second century B.C., but none have survived.

Dr. Hu cited three factors which made for permanence in university life: (1) the college corporation as a property owning and holding organization, (2) an independent self governing faculty free of political control, and (3) the alumni association. The last of these, according to Dr. Hu is "essentially an American contribution" which "probably will play a more and more important part in university life throughout the world ... and may turn out to be the greatest safeguard and guarantor of the freedom of the university ... Alumni associations can help protect the universities by fighting any attempt by the state for control of the university."

President Wilkins, who presided at the luncheon, announced the gift of $25,000 from Mr. R. T. Miller, Jr., '91 to be used for the "further enrichment of the collections" of the Dudley Peter Allen Memorial Art Museum. Dr. Wilkins also announced the acceptance of Harry E. Barnard, '15, of Detroit, Michigan, as a member of the Board of Trustees, following his election the day before.

Other speakers at the luncheon were Thomas E. Harris, '33, who as alumni secretary, welcomed the graduates into the Alumni Association; Donald Emig, senior class president, who responded for the Class of 1942; Mrs. Agnes Warner Mastick, '92, who spoke for the fifty year class; and, Dr. Daniel P. Quiring, '17, who spoke for the twenty-five year class.

Glee Club Founder
Attends Reunion Concert

Jamin Seth Morse, '82, one of the founders of the Men's Glee Club in 1880, of New York City, attended the Reunion Glee Club Concert held May 23. Mr. Morse was introduced by John E. Wirkler, '03' and the Glee Clubs sang, "Why Do The Nations Rage" from the Messiah in his honor. Approximately seventy-five former Glee Club members took part in the concert. Miss Helena Strassberger, '39' was guest soloist.

Shansi Breakfast
Attracts 125 Guests

Miss Frances Cade, '34' executive secretary of the Oberlin-Shansi Memorial Association, who has resigned from her position effective July 1, was the main speaker at the annual Shansi Breakfast at Elmwood, May 24. Speaking on "China Today" Miss Cade told of the emphasis on reconstruction because in the long run this is of more importance than the resistance to the Japanese now.

Albert L. Seely, the chosen representative for 1942, was introduced to

Random snaps of Commencement activities caught, at top, left to right: speakers' table at the Alumni Luncheon, and parade of the reunion classes; second row: the academic procession leaving Peter's Hall with the Reverend Norman Vincent Peale, Baccalaureate Speaker, at extreme left with President Wilkins; and, the Men's Dinner at which Dr. R. P. Jameson, '00, retiring as fencing coach, was presented with a testimonial scroll by Dr. J. H. Nichols, '11, director of athletics.

the group. There was no commissioning service as there is little hope at present of his getting to China at this time. Miss Charlotte Tinker, '37, and Melville Kennedy, '38, and Miss Cade were the only returned representatives present.

Dr. W. F. Bohn, '00, Chairman of the Board of Trustees, presided at the breakfast. Liu En-T'sun, representative of the Ming Hsien Schools, expressed his appreciation of being able to study in the United States and brought greetings from Oberlin-in-China.

Ellsworth Carlson, '39, who was to have come back from China this year has cabled that he will remain with the school for another year.

Arrangements are now in the process of being made to carry on the work of the Shansi Association following Miss Cade's departure.

Senior Class Gift
Goes to Oberlin Center

Members of the Class of 1942 voted that the senior class gift of $150 this year should go to the Phillis Wheatley Community Center in Oberlin. The announcement was made at the class

breakfast held May 25 at which Don Emig, president, presided and Thomas E. Harris, alumni secretary, was the speaker.

Men's Dinner Honors
Dr. R. P. Jameson, '00

Dr. R. P. Jameson, '00, was the honor guest at the Men's Dinner held at the Hi-O-Hi Tea Room during Commencement Week. Dr. Jameson, who is retiring as varsity fencing coach this year, was presented with a testimonial statement by Dr. J. H. Nichols, '11, in behalf of the physical education department.

Dr. Jameson, who was one of Oberlin's first fencers under the late Dr. Fred E. Leonard, '89, reintroduced fencing to Oberlin as an intramural sport in 1929. In 1934 it was put on a varsity basis.

Dean Carl F. Wittke was the guest speaker at the banquet. Alumni golf awards announced by George M. Jones, '94, were as follows: Warren Steller, '19, won his first leg on the President's Cup. John Landis, '20, was runner-up. Dr. C. F. N. Schram, x'08, won the

Merriam Cup for men out more than 25 years and O. M. Walton, '16, was runner-up. Other awards in the tourney went to Andrew Landis, '36, fewest number of putts; Tharon Parsons, '39, for most pars among contestants shooting over 100; and to T. J. Farquhar, '18, and Herbert Gans, T '33, who tied for the least number of putts in the "over 100" division.

With a lack of returning alumni tennis players and with the courts in bad shape the annual alumni-varsity tennis match was called off this year. In the alumni-varsity baseball game the varsity won 6-2. Charles Kent, '40, and John Schwertman, '30, scored for the alumni.

YOUR 1942 ALUMNI

AS OF JUNE

Chairman—Whiting Williams, '99

Steering Committee

Alice Lockwood Andrews, '21
Gertrude Schuchman Engstrom, '18
James H. Griswold, '98
S. Lyle Hudson, '29
Grover H. Hull, '08
John H. Jameson, '18
Marcus M. Kalbfleisch, '16
Fred S. McConnell, '99
Benjamin F. McMahon, '05
Marian Warren Moore, '21
Louis S. Peirce, '28
Carroll K. Shaw, '28

General Secretary

Thomas E. Harris, '33

Classes prior to 1891—
Howard Russell, Agent

1891—Mrs. Grace Stanton Love,
Agent

1892—Mrs. Agnes Warner
Mastick, Agent

1893—Mrs. Edith Cole Shattuck,
Agent

1894—Charles Stocker, Agent
Assistants: Mrs. Harriet Cobb
Anderson, Mrs. Lucy Hoskins Ayres,
John Boss, Mrs. Caroline Ruddock
Holly, Arthur T. Laird, Bernard G.
Mattson, John Mott, Mrs. Louise Hill
Norton, Wilmot E. Stevens, Mrs. Lida
Peck Taylor.

1895—Ernest Partridge, Agent
Assistants: Mrs. Dell Close Jack,
Miss Rose Leiter, Mrs. Winona
Graffam Partridge.

1896—Ethelbert Grabill, Agent

1897—Miss Ethelwyn Charles

1898—Ira Shaw, Agent
Assistants: Miss Bertha Bailey, Miss
Leora Cross, Albert Norris.

1899—Clarence E. Simpson,
Agent
Assistants: Miss Mary A. Cooledge,

Mrs. Nellie Moorhead Dougall,
Clarence Johnson, Mrs. Sarah Browne
MacLennan, Harley Moorhead, Mrs.
Grace Tenney Olsen, Beatty Williams,
Pliny Williamson.

1900—Miss Stella Norton, Agent
Assistants: Miss Elizabeth Adams,
Miss Frances Banta, Seth Buell, Mrs.
Helen Wright Dutton, Mrs. Jessie
Miller Edgerton, DeForest Roe, Bruce
Swift.

1901—Mrs. Mary Day Laird,
Agent
Assistants: Mrs. Frances Stiles
Cheney, Miss Clara Gilbert, John L.
Laird, Walter Lanphear.

1902—Mrs. Alice Charles Reid,
Agent
Assistants: Mrs. Glenna Hostetter
Clark, Mrs. Helen Hough Eaton, Mrs.
Georgia Carrothers Ewing, James
Jewett, Mrs. Helen Chute Lightner,
Orville Sanborn.

1903—Willard Beal, Agent
Assistants: Harvey Heebner, E.
Allan Lightner, Miss Ruth Nichols,
George Pierce, Mrs. Cordelia Ragon
Splitstone.

1904—Howard Rawdon, Agent

1905—Benjamin McMahon,
Agent
Assistants: Mrs. Ruth Savage Cross,
Miss Louise Grove, Ray Howe, D.
Clifford Jones, Mrs. Eva Sweet Kelsey,
Ross Sanderson, Perry Smith.

1906—Emmett Thompson,
Agent

1908—Stanley Kent, Agent

1909—D. Windzor Jones, Agent

1910—Percy Ebbott, Agent
Assistants: Mrs. Mary Hull Baker,
William Clegg, Mrs. Mary Lindsay
Hoffman, Philip King, Mrs. Pearl
Shafer Lickey, Mrs. Fanny Stowell
Loomis, Miss Rhoda McCulloch,
Whitelaw Morrison, Chester Pendle-
ton, Oliver Richards, Rupert Rogers,
Mrs. Ruth Nethercut Rogers, Charles

Shedd, William Smails, George Vradenburg.

1911—Arthur Baker, Agent
Assistants: John Andrews, Mrs.
Helen Wright Avery, G. Henry Birrell,
Miss Dorothy Blake, Mrs. Lulu Acker
Blake, Donald Brodie, Harry Flagal,
Rollin Holbrook, John Kline, Miss
Mabel Law, Mrs. Anna Kauffman
Leate, Will Lyon, W. Arthur McKin-
ney, Aaron Mercer, Keyes Metcalf, J.
Philip Perry, Robert Riggs, Hally
Scott, Frank Tear, Miss Constance
Teeple, Miss Clare Tousley, Thomas
Towle, Miss Hope Vincent, Alfred
Walton, Mrs. Edna Branson Warner.

1912—Hugh Cameron, Agent

1913—Carlos Bushnell, Agent
Assistants: Mrs. Martha Nichols
Blackwell, Mrs. Celia Scoby Clarke,
Mrs. Josephine Wray Fisher, Miss
Juanita Gibson, Mrs. Ruth Newell
Griffith, Miss Marjorie Hamilton,
George Hastings, Miss Mercy Hooker,
Mrs. Laura Helsell Liddell, Lloyd
Mattson, Miss Elizabeth McCloy, J.
Paul Munson, Mrs. Edna Dexter
Niederhauser, Walter Obert, Mrs.
Edith Johnson Schweser.

1914—Leyton Carter, Agent

1915—Mrs. Dana Humphrey
Johnson, Agent
Assistants: Bruce Baxter, Miss Clare
Bell, Mrs. Charlotte Weatherill Bos-
worth, Miss Florence Burger, Mrs.
Ruth Richardson Cowdery, Howard
Curtis, Miss Margaret Doerschuk,
Philip Gott, Miss Anna May Hughes,
Miss Pearle Lennox, Nathan Mack,
Herbert Mayer, Carlton Matson, Mrs.
Ursul Reeves Moran, Mrs. Grace
Foster Rothrock.

1916—Mrs. Hannah Witkop
Kellogg, Agent

1917—Miss Mary E. Andrews,
Agent
Assistants: Mrs. Hyacinthe Scott
Baker, Mrs. Naomi Henry Little, Mrs.
Helen Ludwig Nelson, Miss Arelisle
Quimby, Mrs. Florence Erickson Tone.

FUND ORGANIZATION

FIFTEENTH   Vice Chairman—Ruth Tracy Millard, '28

1918—Robert Judson, Agent

1919—Mrs. Katherine Kilmer Farquhar, Agent

1920—Mrs. Helen Drew Greensmith, Agent

Assistants: George Bent, Mrs. Elizabeth Crofts Callison, Mrs. Marian Lawrence Hester, Miss Elizabeth Pape, Miss Helen Paulison.

1921—Mrs. Alice Lockwood Andrews, Agent

1922—C. Raymond Clipson, Agent

Assistants: Mrs. Muriel Easton Adams, Sherman Brown, Maxwell Hahn, R. Jack Herberts, Mrs. Mildred Mickey Hutchinson, Dewey Olson.

1923—Mrs. Marion Downing Andrews, Agent

Assistants: Mrs. Geraldine Ford Holcomb, Gilbert Robinson, Mrs. Norma Dyer Swearingen, Mrs. Ruth Williams Taggart, Mrs. Etha Peabody Waddell, Miss Marjorie Warner.

1924—Irvin Houck, Agent

1925—Victor Obenhaus, Agent

1926—Robert Fisher, Agent

Assistants: Miss Elizabeth Bennett, Mrs. Martha Stiles Booth, Mrs. Elinor Cook Bushnell, Mrs. Virginia White Croxton, Frank deVyver, Clarmont Doane, Mrs. Anna Creighton Harbourt, Mrs. Marion Green Harrar, Francis Holbein, Mrs. Louise Poole Johnson, J. Howard McMillen, Mrs. Maren Thomsen Stewart, Paul Titus.

1927—Edwin Howe, Agent

1928—Richard Schaefer, Agent

1929—C. Francis Alter, Agent

1930—Thomas Williams, Agent

Assistants: Miss Mary Beattie, Alfred Churchill, Mrs. Martha Rugh Platt.

1931—Robert Barr, Agent

Assistants: Mrs. Mary Dann

Bohlmann, Donald Bowland, Brainerd Bridgman, Charles Canfield, Miss Carolyn Dann, Mrs. Marjorie Watters Fischer, Miss Ida Flickinger, Jared Ford, William Griffiths, George Harwood, Mrs. Roselle Bezazian Kemalyan, Miss Irene Kline, Miss Grace Leslie, Yngve Olsen, Mrs. Dorothy Butler Smith, Miss Pauline Wallace.

1932—Richard Davis, Agent

Assistants: William Adams, Ellwyn Bails, Mrs. Jane Randle Banks, Ralph Burry, Donald Church, Mrs. Amy Kremers Hill, Mrs. Helen Horton McCaa, Miss Katharine McCullough, Mrs. Marian Channell Ross, F. Champion Ward, Mrs. Antoinette Claypoole Wood.

1933—Mrs. Jean Boyd Jones, Agent

Assistants: Mrs. Elizabeth Fauver Bischoff, John Brown, Warren Cameron, Mrs. Lillian Hill Cheney, Karl Cowdery, Mrs. Edith Williams Davies, Mrs. Lois Russell Franz, Miss Helen Grant, Mrs. Jean Young Gratz, A. Clarence Hall, Miss Eleanor Hamm, Mrs. Eone Goodenough Harger, Mrs. Elizabeth Stratton Hawley, Glenn Lewis, Dean Lightener, Miss Florence Materse, Miss Sarah Metcalf, Miss Margaret Ping, Miss Dorothy Rainer, Wade Smith, William Steigely, Mrs. Marian Harger Stewart, R. Richard Wieland.

1934—Dana Whitmer, Agent

Assistants: Angelo Dublo, Frank Engelhart, Mrs. Helen Edwards Laird, William McRae, Thomas Williams.

1935—Mrs. Virginia Burrett Shepard, Agent

Assistants: Mrs. Marian Zannoth Green, Miss Jean Kinsey, Mrs. Elizabeth Bowen Morse, Mrs. Alice Pfund Urist.

1936—Richard Aszling, Agent

Assistants: Miss Frances Eddy, E. John Hamlin, Atlee Zellers.

1937—Frederick Brewster, Agent

Assistants: Mrs. Suzanne Rohn Ballard, John Belding, Miss Janice

Publicity Committee

Percy J. Ebbott, '10
Claire MacMurray Howard, x'21
John H. Wieland, '29

Regional Advisors

Earl F. Adams, '01'
New Haven, Conn.
Marguerite Wenk Curtis, '10'
Denver, Colo.
Louis E. Hart, '93
Chicago, Ill.
Edward P. Millikan, '20'
San Francisco, Calif.
Helen Morrison Riggs, '12'
Tulsa, Okla.
Augusta Jewitt Street, '11'
Richmond, Va.

Carkin, Miss Virginia Deringer, Lawrence Gill, Mrs. Elizabeth Hammond Holdeman, Miss Lois Goodenough Peterson, Walter Richards, Mrs. Jeanne Lesser Richards, Miss Elizabeth Strawbridge, Herbert Van Meter, Harold Zaugg.

1938—James Deer, Agent

1939—Miss Dorothy Eberhart, Agent

1940—Miss Elizabeth Byron, Agent

Assistants: O. Willard Bidwell, Miss Lota Brandt, Avery Fisher, Miss Phyllis Frost, Miss Esther Gott, Miss Doris Leith, Miss Bessie Massing, Miss Mary Root, Mrs. Georgia Maxwell Wegman.

1941—Mrs. Sara Atkinson Snyder, Agent

Assistants: Miss Lois Baker, Miss Irene Diefenbach, Robert Fleischer, Miss Margaret Hitchner, Jack Hume, Miss Ann Jewett, Miss Lois Keller, Robert Lewis, Miss Elizabeth Manson, Ad Mueller, Richard Ruggles, Miss Wynne Wolf.

Left to right: Honorary Marshall Archer H. Shaw, '97, Dr. David Mannes, Dr. Hu Shih, President Wilkins, Dr. Raymond H. Stetson, '93, Dr. Paul H. Fall, '14, and, Dr. George H. Sabine.

HONORARY DEGREES

Two Oberlin alumni were among the five recipients of honorary degrees at the 109th Anniversary Commencement exercises. Dr. Raymond H. Stetson, '93, M.A. '96, emeritus head of the Psychology Department, was granted the Doctor of Science degree. Dr. Paul H. Fall, '14, M.A. '18, president of Hiram College, received the Doctor of Laws degree. The other degree awards were His Excellency Hu Shih, Chinese Ambassador to the United States, Doctor of Laws; David Mannes, violinist and co-director of the David Mannes Music School of New York City, Doctor of Music; and, Dr. George H. Sabine, dean of the Graduate School, Cornell University, Doctor of Letters.

The presentation of candidates, and citations, follow:

Raymond H. Stetson

Presentation by Professor Hartson:

Mr. President: It is my privilege to present to you an alumnus, who, as a member of the faculty, has built his spirit into the structure of Oberlin College.

Prepared for his specialization in psychology by a rich experience as student and teacher in the natural sciences, modern languages, the arts and philosophy, his classroom was vitalized by a wealth of illustration which served to provoke the thought and broaden the imagination of his students.

He built a department of psychology unique for its interest in scientific inquiry; a fact attested, at the time of his retirement from active teaching, by a *Festschrift*, reporting research work by some of his students. It was this interest in creative investigation, permeating the policy of the institution, which led to the recognition of Oberlin as one of a half dozen liberal arts colleges in the country worthy of being granted a chapter of Sigma Xi. His colleagues considered it appropriate that he should serve as the first president of the chapter.

His own investigations in the field of phonetics, supported by basic studies in the analysis of skilled movements, have been described as "probably the most fundamental research in this field being carried on in this country." International recognition of the significance of this work is evidenced by the choice of his monograph, *Motor Phonetics*, as a yearbook of the Association Néerlandaise des Sciences Phonétiques, and by his election as the American member of the council of The International Congress of Phonetic Sciences.

The qualities which have made possible these scientific achievements—thoroughness of preparation, intensity of purpose, passion for facts, utter disinterestedness, devotion to truth, abhorrence of all that falls short of absolute honesty and integrity—have likewise characterized his personal influence. The force of these qualities, throughout his years of service, have done much to determine the standards of scholarship of present-day Oberlin.

Mr. President, I am happy to present Raymond Herbert Stetson for the degree of Doctor of Science.

Citation by President Wilkins:

Raymond Herbert Stetson, scientist par excellence, analyst of the motion that is life, Leonardo turned at last psychologist, the degree of Doctor of Science.

Paul H. Fall

Presentation by Professor Holmes:

Mr. President, the alumnus whom you have called back to honor on this occasion is accustomed to return engagements.

Hiram College, after allowing him two years' absence to complete the requirements for the doctor's degree at Cornell University, gladly insisted on his returning to continue his excellent work in building up their department of chemistry. Williams College was so well pleased with his year there as Visiting Professor that, a few years later, they invited him to become a permanent member of their faculty.

Not to be outdone in such expressions of confidence, Hiram College, three years later, elected him as their President at the unanimous and enthusiastic request of their faculty. Thereupon, as an evidence of good will, Williams College conferred upon him the LL.D. degree.

His honors are richly deserved, for in him you find marked ability as chemist, teacher and executive; integrity and sincerity; contagious enthusiasm and the qualities of inspiring leadership. To call him a typical Oberlin alumnus would indeed be honoring his Alma Mater.

Mr. President, I take deep personal pleasure in presenting for the degree of Doctor of Laws one of Oberlin's distinguished sons, President of Hiram College, Dr. Paul Henry Fall of the Class of 1914 and Master of Arts of 1918.

Citation by President Wilkins:

Paul Henry Fall, chemist administrant, faithful in each enlarging trust, seeking now the high alchemy of educational transmutation, the degree of Doctor of Laws.

His Excellency Hu Shih

Presentation by Dr. Bohn:

Mr. President: There stands before you a Son of the East who, representing the world's largest republic, is, literally and officially, designated as "The great Emissary of the Flowery People's Country of the Middle,"—but who in his own personal right represents the flower of a race and a culture which counts its thousands of years more easily than we do our hundreds. In his own person he is the incarnation of those qualities and achievements of the Chinese people which have astonished the whole world and because of which

China, a non-military nation abhorring the arts and machinations of aggressive war, has nevertheless been able to hold the line of Freedom and Human Rights through years of conflict.

In the development of that culture he has played a major role, and it is not evaluating his achievements too highly to link with the name of Sun Yat-sen, the Founder of the Republic, that of the Scholar and Philosopher, hailed as the "Father of the Chinese Renaissance' for his revitalizing of the Chinese language and the dignifying "as literature the popular speech of his time and place."

At the age of three he knew eight hundred characters of the Chinese written language and was humorously called" The Master" by his playmates. Before he was thirty he was acknowledged the foremost philosopher of modern China. While avoiding the entanglements of official life for twenty years and still, even today, insisting, "I have degenerated into an Ambassador"—nevertheless, at perhaps the greatest crisis in our American history, last December, his ambassadorial qualities "held China and the United States together and was the greatest triumph of his career."

Mr. President, I have the honor of presenting to you an exponent and a creator of a great culture and a great literature, an interpreter and a maker of history, a loyal patriot and a citizen of the world, America's Friend and Ally, Dr. Hu—His Excellency, the Ambassador of the Republic of China.

Citation by President Wilkins:

His Excellency Hu Shih, envoy of ancient and of modern nobility, welder of international bonds that are stronger than death, prophet of a multinational democratic unity that shall be resolute for the welfare of all men, and shall be wreathed with learning, the degree of Doctor of Laws.

George H. Sabine

Presentation by Dean Wittke:

A native son of Ohio, George Holland Sabine was educated to the degree of Doctor of Philosophy at Cornell University. He is a member of both Phi Beta Kappa and Sigma Xi. His notable career as a teacher of philosophy began at Leland Stanford. By slow stages, after seven years at Stanford, nine at Missouri, and eight at Ohio State University, he made his academic way back to his Alma Mater, where he is now professor of philosophy, faculty representative on the Board of Trustees, and Dean of the Graduate School.

Wherever he has been, his remarkable common sense and his keen ability to make objective analyses of men and situations insured his being drafted for administrative tasks, and he has left the

mark of his educational statesmanship on the curriculum and procedures of all the universities he has served.

An excellent classicist, an authority on certain phases of mediaeval thought, and one of the outstanding philosophers of our generation, Dr. Sabine has published with distinction in all these fields. But his *History of Political Theory*, an outstanding single volume presentation of political and ethical concepts from antiquity to the present day, perhaps best reveals the stature of the scholar and the man, and his close intellectual kinship with the Greeks whose institutions have been a favorite subject of his scholarship. Here are to be found the origins of our modern concepts of justice, liberty and law, freedom of discussion and constitutional government. To the study, dissemination, and defense of these fundamental values, on and off the campus, Professor Sabine's career has been unflinchingly devoted.

Mr. President, I have the honor to present George Holland Sabine for the degree of Doctor of Letters.

Citation by President Wilkins:

George Holland Sabine, lover of that wisdom which is indeed the guide of life, teacher and champion of the philosophy of freedom, the degree of Doctor of Letters.

David Mannes

Presentation by Professor Hall:

The career of David Mannes has been centered in the city of his birth, New York. Indeed, he has become one of the strongest and most wholesome musical forces in that great city.

For some twenty years he was a violinist in the New York Symphony Orchestra, during fourteen of those years its concert-master. The more intimate world of chamber music has been deeply enriched by his sensitive interpretations. Gifted with great imagination and a passion to share with others his love of music, David Mannes welcomed the opportunity to teach violin to the music-hungry children of the New York Music School Settlement. Even before he terminated his fifteen years of association with that great school, with the true spirit of the missionary, he had founded in Harlem the Music Settlement for Colored People. He has aided in the establishment of music settlements for all races throughout this country. For a number of years Mr. Mannes has served as a Trustee of Fisk University.

In the direction of The Mannes Music School, founded in 1916, there has been illustrated the rare combination of keen powers of administration joined to sensitive artistic insight. Not only has this school sent forth professional performers, composers and

teachers, but its doors have always been open to "amateurs of all ages and capacities." This breadth of sympathy and love of the people, this desire to bring music to all, runs like a *leitmotiv* through Mr. Mannes' life. Still another illustration is found in his work as a conductor. His vision of concerts with no economic or social barriers has been realized in a series of concerts given every season since 1918 at the Metropolitan Museum of Art; more than a million have been spiritually refreshed as David Mannes has recreated the music of the great composers. His highly interesting autobiography is titled *Music is My Faith.*

Through his faith, as a violinist, conductor and educator, David Mannes has lead the world closer to that which is "good, just, and beautiful." I have the honor, Mr. President, to present to you for the degree of Doctor of Music, David Mannes.

Citation by President Wilkins:

David Mannes, mankind his violin and faith his bow, gladdener of the still, sad music of humanity, the degree of Doctor of Music.

Father's Raise $1100 For Scholarships

Some time ago, at the suggestion of the father of a freshman student, a plan was conceived for providing a modest Scholarship Fund each year, to be known as the Fathers' Scholarship Fund, to meet special emergencies arising in the present war situation and in the normal course of college work for certain students of limited financial resources. The proposal met with immediate and enthusiastic response and a fund of $1100 was provided, with an intimation on the part of some of those who contributed that they would be glad to continue participation in this plan in years to come. This result guarantees that enough will be paid in to meet emergency situations in a number of cases this summer and through next year which might otherwise result in educational tragedies.

Lahaurine-Johnston Prize Awards Made

First awards of the Lahaurine-Johnston Prizes were made late in May to Edith Shipherd and Harry Otis, both seniors. The prizes, valued at $15 each, were from the fund established in memory of the late Madame Marie-Jeanne Lahaurine-Johnston, former directrice de la Maison Francaise, and were made in recognition of what the committee considered the most persistent use of the facilities of French House. Alice James, '42' received a medal given by the French Consulate in Philadelphia for the best work in French this year.

REUNIONS...

Class of 1877

Two representatives of the Class of 1877 celebrated the 65th anniversary of their graduation this year. They were Mrs. Emelie Royce Comings of Oberlin and Mrs. Anna Mead Hobbs of Lakewood.

Class of 1891

While it was not a special reunion year for the class, there were eight present at Commencement time and several interesting social affairs were arranged. On Sunday evening they were guests of Mrs. Minnie Beard Siddall for supper at her home. Later in the evening there were calls from six of the eight holders of the '91 scholarships: Evelyn Bliss, Caspar, Wyoming; Robert Boyle, Seattle, Washington; Gwendolyn Freeman, Paterson, New Jersey; Betty May Hertzler, Lincoln, Nebraska; Wilton Nichols, Cleveland; and Gerald Smith, Chicago. Colored films sent by George and Gertrude Wilder, now in Peking, were shown, as well as some campus scenes.

On Monday there was a luncheon at Cranford, the 'reunion' home of the class. Dr. and Mrs. Cairns joined the party for luncheon. The members of the class present were Mrs. Rose Hunter Carpenter, Miss Edith Clarke, Mrs. Alice Jones Emery, Mrs. Carrie Memmott Lawrence, Mrs. Grace Stanton Love. Mr. R. T. Miller, Jr., Mrs. Minnie Beard Siddall, and Mr. Jarvis Strong. Following luncheon there was an informal exchange of the latest news of the class. At the Alumni luncheon on Tuesday announcement was made of another gift of $25,000 from Mr. R. T. Miller, Jr., the money to be used for the purchase of works of art for the Allen Art Museum.

Class of 1892

Seventy-five graduated in the class of 1892. Of the 35 living members, 16 were in Oberlin for the 50 year reunion. The faded '92 flag was hung in front of the headquarters at Elmwood Cottage and was an invitation to old friends to call. Old photographs and souvenirs from college days down-helped revive memories of the fifty years. Every meal was a reunion, but the heart of the reunion was the class supper Sunday evening at the new home of Mr., '90' and Mrs. Allan F. Millikan (Mary Plumb, '93) when 34 gathered at the hospitable board. At the roll-call there was a message, either direct or indirect, from every member of the class. At the close of the meeting Dr. William J.

Hutchins, who was a former member, read the names of the 12 classmates who had died since the reunion five years ago and made a prayer of thanksgiving for the continuing fellowship.

Mrs. Mary Farnsworth Ransom was elected class representative on the Alumni Council. Mrs. Agnes Warner Mastick spoke for the class at the Alumni luncheon.

The following members were present Mrs. Doris McMaster Bibbins, Mrs. Jean Beatty Bowman, Mrs. Josephine Paige Burr, Dr. Scott P. Child, Mrs. Mary Francis Evans, Miss Louie A. Hall, Dr. Lynds Jones, Mrs. Agnes Warner Mastick, Mr. Chester F. Ralston, Mrs. Mary Farnsworth Ransom, Mr. Crawford L. Smith, Mrs. Inez Michener Smith, Miss Cora L. Swift, Mrs. Ella Dudley Walker, Mr. Frank N. Williams, and Dr. Stephen R. Williams.

Class of 1897

Twenty members of the Class of 1897 with their husbands, wives and children returned for their forty-fifth reunion held at Shurtleff Cottage. Following the dinner on Baccalaureate Sunday several letters from absent classmates were read including one from Edith Brand Hannah in England. The class then resolved into a court with Mr. Daniel E. Morgan, judge of the court of appeals, presiding. Vernon O. Johnston, acting as attorney before the court of appeals, presented a formal petition of adoption of Clair McMurray Howard, the first child born of a '97 parent. Mrs. Howard is the daughter of Mrs. Kathryn Romig McMurray and the late James H. McMurray. The petition was signed by all the members of the class. Mrs. Howard in a speech expressing her gratitude complimented the Class of '97 on their personal appearance. "What a pretty bunch you are," she said.

Members of '92 attending were Miss Frances Bement, Mrs. Emma Hutchins Burt, Miss Ethelwyn Charles, Mrs. Grace Erwin Curtiss, Dr. Harlan Dudley, Dr. William D. Ferguson, Dr. Clifford Gilmore, Miss Florence Fitch, Mr. Everett P. Johnson, Mr. Vernon Johnston, Dr. Louis Lord, Mr. Henry C. Marshall, Mr. Daniel E. Morgan, Miss Harriet Penfield, Miss Ellen R. Raymond, Mr. and Mrs. Edward A. Seibert (Jessie White), Dr. Arthur G. Thatcher, Miss Mabel P. Wetterling, Mrs. Edna Randolph White, Miss Manetta Marsh, and Mr. Archer H. Shaw.

Class of 1907

The Class of 1907 held its 35th reunion at the Oberlin Inn on Sunday. After a chicken dinner and a business meeting at which it was decided to buy a bond with funds in the treasury and officers were reelected, the group adjourned to a private parlor where Dr. Ruth Parmelee told us of her work in Greece under the American Women's Hospitals. Letters from other class members were read and a jolly friendly good time was shared by the 26 members, wives and husbands present.

Class of 1912

Two gatherings occupied the members of 1912 at Commencement. Mrs. Esther Andrews Johnson entertained 32 members of the class at her home Saturday evening, and on Sunday the group held their reunion dinner at the Graystone Hotel in Elyria. At a business meeting after the dinner Mrs. Johnson was elected reunion chairman and Mrs. Adele Brown was named class counselor.

Class of 1916

Although not a reunion year 25 members of the Class of 1916 gathered in Oberlin and were entertained by Mrs. Wilda Bunce Jones at her home on Sunday evening.

Class of 1917

The Class of 1917, first to graduate into World War I, held its 25th reunion in a world even more chaotic than that of its graduation day. Uncertainties regarding the entire Commencement program at Oberlin, as well as upset conditions in the lives of the members of the class, forced a somewhat impromptu program for the reunion. Through Saturday evening seven or eight of us rattled around loosely at May Cottage, our headquarters, rather dolefully asserting that we would never come back for another reunion.

Sunday brought a happy surprise. Into town began to troop the members of the class. It was suggested that we have some of our former teachers for dinner. Luckily we were able to corral Dr. and Mrs. Holmes, Dr. and Mrs. Rogers, Dr. and Mrs. Hubbard, Dr. and Mrs. Jelliffe, Dr. and Mrs. Cairns, and Dr. Stetson. When we sat down to dinner there were seventy-nine of us, including class "in-laws" who for all practical purposes belong to the class. (Betty Schuchman's husband has hung around Oberlin meetings so much that he almost got himself elected president of the Pittsburgh chapter. He was caught in time.) Following the dinner, more classmates came in, until there was scarcely standing room in the lounges at May. One of the great pleasures of the occasion was that of

Class of 1907

The Class of 1907 held its reunion, at the Oberlin Inn on Saturday. After a chicken dinner and a short meeting at which it was decided that a fund worth funds it should be... officers were reelected, the group of Ruth Parmelee told us of her work in Greece under the American Women's Hospitals. Letters from other class members were read and a jolly friendly good time was shared by the 26 members, wives and husbands present.

Class of 1912

Two gatherings occupied the members of 1912 at Commencement. Mrs. Esther Andrews Johnson entertained 15 members of the class at her home Saturday evening, and on Sunday the group held their reunion dinner at the Graystone Hotel in Elyria. At a business meeting after the dinner Mrs. Johnson was elected reunion chairman and Mrs. Adele Brown was named class counselor.

Class of 1916

Although not a reunion year 21 members of the Class of 1916 gathered in Oberlin and were entertained by Mrs. Wilda Bunce Jones at her home on Sunday evening.

Class of 1917

The Class of 1917, first to graduate into World War I, held its 25th reunion in a world even more chaotic than that of its graduation day. Conditions regarding the peace Commencement program in Oberlin, is well as upset conditions in the lives of the members of the class, forced a somewhat impromptu program for the reunion. Through Saturday evening seven or eight of us rattled around loosely at May Cottage, our headquarters, rather dolefully averring that we would never come back for another reunion.

Sunday brought a happier aspect...

meeting some of the children of our classmates and of other college friends.

At the dinner, in partial answer to such all-to-frequent questions as, "Where is Jack? Why didn't Mary come?" and "Have you heard anything about Bill?" Notes and letters from various absent members were read. It was the consensus of those present that the 25th reunion was such a success in spirit, if not in numbers, that it must be repeated in both spirit and numbers at a later date. Therefore, the class voted to hold another 25th reunion in 1947, and through the ill-will of Percy Johnson and his aides, Ross Marvin was saddled with the job of gauleiter for 1947. The class also voted to have a report of the reunion prepared and sent to all members. What's more important, they dipped into their pockets and raised the cash for the job.

MacConnachie Named
Senior Class President

Gordon MacConnachie, '43, of Montclair, New Jersey, was named president of his class for next year at elections held in May. Other class presidents elected were Richard Hoar, '44, of Akron and Bruce Marshall, '45, of Youngstown. Hoar is the son of John M. Hoar, '17. Wilson Bent, son of Mr., '20 and Mrs. George R. Bent (Eleanor Hopkins, '22), was named men's social chairman of the Class of '45.

Reunion classes gathered at Oberlin for the 109th Commencement include, top: Class of 1917; second row, left to right: Class of 1897, and Class of 1892; bottom row, left to right: Class of 1902 and Class of 1877 represented by Mrs. Emelie Royce Comings of Oberlin, and Mrs. Anna Mead Hobbs of Lakewood.

Show Hall Movie
At Apollo Theatre

"Unfinished Rainbows," the motion picture about aluminum and Charles M. Hall's contribution to its commercial use, was shown at the Apollo Theatre during Commencement Week for the benefit of the returning alumni.

IN RECOGNITION OF---

Louis Peirce, '28, Retires As Alumni President

For three years Louis Peirce has guided the policy of the Alumni Association as its president. In retiring this June he can look back upon those years as successful ones because of the energy and hard work which he himself put into it. Mr. Peirce has served many Oberlin organizations both as an undergraduate and as an alumnus, but his years as president of the Association have been a real and valued service to the College. Under his direction the Alumni Fund program has been developed in detail. It was through his initiative and leadership that arrangements were effected for the present cooperative relationship between the College administration and the Association with respect to fund raising activities. This one development of the past year offers promise of a greater Alumni Association than Oberlin has ever had and one of greater service to the College.

As a member of the class of 1928 Mr. Peirce was chairman of the Mock Convention, president of the Senior Class and a member of Phi Beta Kappa. After graduating from Oberlin he attended Harvard Law School where he was on the Harvard *Law Review*. He then became associated with the law firm of Tolles, Hogsett & Ginn in Cleveland. Later he became counsel for the Regional Office of the Securities and Exchange Commission of Cleveland. He is active in local organizations— trustee of the Legal Aid Society, a director of the Foreign Affairs Council, a trustee of the Humane Society and vice president of the Harvard Club of Cleveland.

In 1937 he was elected chairman of the junior council of the Alumni Association and under his leadership the junior council was very active and proposed a number of policies later adopted by the Association. The most important was the new method of electing the Alumni trustee. It was his unusual capacity for direction of a group that made him the logical candidate for president of the Association in 1939. It was with some reluctance that he accepted the presidency, for at this time he was just undertaking the new responsibilities as general counsel and secretary of the National Refining Company in Cleveland. He knew that his new position would make heavy demands upon his time and energy, but such was his interest in Oberlin Alumni affairs that he undertook the duties of president of the Alumni Association.

Not long after the full responsibilities of the executive direction of his company fell upon his shoulders when two top officials were in an airplane accident. It would have been easy for him to drop the affairs of the Association, and under the circumstances he would have been justified, but his unfailing loyalty to Oberlin and his intense desire to make the Association program a success led him to continue the active leadership of its affairs. In spite of his own work he was always ready to give his best thought and planning to the Association.

When on last December 8th Carroll Shaw, alumni secretary, resigned to take a position in Washington, the task of selecting a new secretary and revising the plans of the Alumni Fund Campaign added immeasurably to the work of Mr. Peirce. It necessitated many meetings and endless correspondence since the members of his executive committee came from New York, Detroit, Chicago, and Cleveland.

As the war developed each meeting meant the discarding of previous plans and starting all over again. But under his leadership the committee was convinced that there was a place for the Association in this emergency as well as an opportunity to serve the College through its young men who would soon be called to war. During this trying time his ability to guide the committee without imposing his own ideas on others and yet arrive at a workable answer to the various problems was remarkable. Carroll Shaw once expressed it thus. "I am always impressed with the meticulous way in which at the close of a protracted discussion of a problem in committee, he reviews the various points raised by each of the members before he calls for a vote on a question. That summarization helps clarify the thinking of all those present."

George M. Jones, '94, Awarded Alumni Medal

George M. Jones, '94, emeritus-secretary of the College, was named the ninth recipient of the Alumni Medal for Notable Service at the annual meeting of the Alumni Association, May 24. The presentation of the medal was made by Louis Peirce, Alumni Association president. The citation was as follows:

"For more than forty-five years the recipient of this year's Alumni Award served Oberlin College with that disinterested loyalty to a great cause which Walter Lippmann cites in his *Preface to Morals* as the greatest human virtue. Seeking nothing for himself, but desir-

Alumni Association President Louis Peirce, '28, presents the Alumni Medal for Notable Service to Oberlin to Secretary-Emeritus George M. Jones, '94.

ing always to further the interests of the College, he built solidly and well.

"As Secretary of the Board of Trustees and of the Faculty, he was more than a faithful keeper of the records. He saw in those records an architect's plan for a growing institution, the foundation upon which new plans and projects would have to be built if they were to stand.

"As Admissions Officer for many years, he ushered thousands of Freshmen into Oberlin, viewing them all as potential Alumni and friends of the College. In a very real sense he is the builder of the present active constituency of Oberlin.

"As registrar of the alumni lists and editor of the several publications of those lists, he was more than the recorder of changing addresses. He realized that in that great body of information there lay the basis of a powerful cooperative movement between the Alumni and the College,— a two way channel by which the influence of the institution could continue to reach its constituency, and by which the Alumni could find natural and effective ways of contributing to the life of the College from their own rich and growing experience.

"To have stood in such an influential and serviceable relationship to the College and to the Alumni Body for so long a period of time, and to have kept himself constantly in the role of servant to the greater good, is to have richly deserved the recognition of which this award is the symbol.

"I am particularly pleased to bestow the Alumni Award for Notable Service to Oberlin upon George M. Jones."

BOOK SHELF

The Soviets Expected It. By Anna Louise Strong, '05' 279 pages. The Dial Press. 1941. $2.50.

This book is one of a class which includes Joseph E. Davies' *Mission to Moscow*, and Walter Duranty's *The Kremlin and The People*—books written by competent authorities well-disposed toward Russia. Although produced independently and having different approaches they confirm one another in all essential matters. Out of full knowledge of and unusual experience in the Soviet Union and with singular unanimity these authors write so convincingly of the Soviets that the effect will be to dissipate much ignorance and prejudice about Russia. They are books which all Americans may profitably read.

Miss Strong's volume makes clear how the Soviet people prepared morally, politically, industrially, technically and militarily for this war which they knew was coming. She tells how they became devoted to ideals of freedom which have given a morale that will not crack, how the fifth column was eliminated, munition plants built beyond enemy reach, western frontiers recreated as danger approached and conflict staved off as long as possible. The story is told directly, compactly and with ease and charm.

If the author chooses to offer no criticisms of Soviet policy and practice, the reason seems to be that the positive achievements are so overwhelming and significant for the future of mankind that any shortcomings may well be overlooked at least for the present.

This is a justifiable attitude and far more realistic, as the reviewer from first-hand knowledge of Russian conditions can testify, than is the viewpoint of such bitter extremists and irrational critics as Eugene Lyons, Freda Utley, and W. H. Chamberlin, whose distorted reports have made Russia out to be a tragic failure. The facts, however, are coming to light with the Soviets' resistence to the Nazi scourge, and these facts are giving the lie to the critics and the truth to the interpreters of Miss Strong's class.

Newell L. Sims

Metcalf, Franklin P., '13' *Flora of Fukien and Florestic Notes on Southeastern China*, Lingnan University, 1942: First Fascicle.

The first part of an important work on the Flora of Fukien and adjoining provinces of southeastern China by Dr.

Franklin P. Metcalf, '13' has just been published by Lingnan University, Canton, China.

This is the first work to deal comprehensively with the flora of this region. To it Dr. Metcalf has devoted nearly 20 years of intensive study, during which time he has published more than 70 articles on the flora of southeastern China. He is recognized as one of the foremost authorities on the flora of that area.

Fukien province whose flora has been most intensively studied by Dr. Metcalf, is considerably larger than the State of Ohio, while the entire region covered has roughly the area, shape and topography of the eastern United States from northern New England to southern Georgia, westward to the eastern edge of Ohio and Kentucky. However, the region lies in the same latitude as the middle section of Mexico, and its flora, extremely rich and diversified, consists of both subtropical and temperate plants.

In the preparation of this work Dr. Metcalf and his collaborators have not only themselves made very extensive collections in Fukien and nearby provinces, but he has examined critically most of the plants previously collected, which are in the famous herbaria and museums of China, Europe and the United States. The critical evaluation of such diversified and scattered material has required unusually discriminating judgment, wide bibliographical knowledge and the utmost exactitude.

The result is a book for the specialist and for the ordinary student as well. Its completion has required unbounded enthusiasm and untiring energy. The work is a notable achievement.

Frederick Grover

Hulbert, Archer Butler, and Hulbert, Dorothy Printup, '15' *Marcus Whitman-Crusader* (Part III, 1843-1847). The Stewart Commission of Colorado College and the Denver Public Library, Denver, Colorado. 1941. 265 pp. Index. $5.00.

As a scholarly epic to the courage, diplomacy and tragic end of the Pacific slope's most important and probably least known frontier statesman, *Marcus Whitman-Crusader*, the last of a three part exposition of Oregon's history, by Archer and Dorothy Hulbert is a fascinating panorama of a tragedy's causes and brutal enactment.

In handling the ponderous mass of detail the authors cleverly clothe the

specific exactness of history in the warm intriguing hominess of the intimate—withall, maintaining an atmosphere of impending, irresistable murder. One is conscious of the obvious denouement from the first, yet prayerfully hopeful of an escape from the ghastly martyrdom the kindly doctor and his brood suffer at the hands of those whom they had befriended most.

Vividly portrayed are the Whitman's personal life and conduct, as the doctor ponders the three-fold problem: "(1) to quiet the pugnacious Cayuse and their allies while the American migration passed through their lands, bringing the very destruction which these Indians most feared; (2) to aid in every conceivable way that migration and guard, as best he could, the infant settlements below from savage raids; and, (3) to prevent any campaign of revenge for innumerable insults that thoughtless white men in those feeble settlements might make against the Indians, before the Willamette section was too strong to be in danger."

To complement and complete their exacting scholarship, an intriguing collection of letters are included by the authors, letters exchanged with the master of Waiilatpu, who broke the trail for Oregon's settlement and the establishment of the 49th parallel as the northern United States boundary, and his friends and advisors. The letters make up a large part of this historical masterpiece which brings the zest, danger and power to your surprised and pleased attention.

G. H. S.

Notices of recent alumni books include the following: *Yukon Trail* by William M. Raine, '94' Blue Ribbon Books; *Building Morale* by Dr. Jay B. Nash, '11' A. S. Barnes; and, *Critical Theory and Practice of the Pléide* by Robert J. Clements, '34' Harvard Studies in Romance Languages.

Professor William S. Ament, '10' of Scripps College, Claremont, California, is one of the contributors to *The Personalist*, a quarterly journal of philosophy and religion and literature, for April. This issue is devoted to William James in observance of the centenary of his birth. Professor Ament's article is titled, "William James as a Man of Letters."

* * *

Dr. William Lytle Schurz, '04-'05' assistant chief of the Division of Cultural Relations of the State Department, is the author of *Latin America* published by E. P. Dutton in 1941. The book review section of *Advance* says in part: "This book of 378 pages is the result of thirty years of travel,

Continued on page 24

Dr. Karl Gehrkens

Among the twelve thousand definitions of musical terms which Karl Gehrkens edited for Webster's *New International Dictionary*, it may well be that his favorite is that of *Anticipation*. The final chord of the Oberlin teacher's *Magnum Opus* is normally reached at 65, but this Dr. Gehrkens has anticipated by five years. The choice of his career was a happy anticipation, for he was among the first who visioned and realized the wider and deeper field of music education in the public schools. The momentary discords that result when tones are sounded before their time, have had their parallel in the life of Karl Gehrkens; often school boards, committees, and faculties conservatively held to one pattern while Dr. Gehrkens, sensing the "shape of things to come" persistently pressed forward to the rightful resolution.

It was while Dr. Gehrkens was teaching academic subjects in the Oberlin High School following his graduation from Oberlin College in 1905, that he decided to combine his love of music with his work in education. For many years he served as supervisor of music in the Public Schools of the village and at the same time he built the Department of School Music in the Oberlin Conservatory. By stages the department expanded from a two term course to one of four years leading to the degree of Bachelor of School Music. This last advance, accomplished in 1921, may be noted as one of the major steps in American musical education. The curriculum adopted was that which had been formulated by the Research Council of Music Education in which Dr. Gehrkens had been the chief proponent for a healthy balance between courses in

Continued on page 19

Dr. Oscar Jaszi

With the retirement of Oscar Jaszi the moral and intellectual level of Oberlin stands lower. Born in Hungary, he had, before he came to Oberlin in 1925, already completed in his native land a distinguished career as scholar and statesman. His American colleagues and students were, at once, charmed by the delightful humor and the beautiful courtesy of the new professor. Since then four college generations have felt his influence. None of his students will ever forget the strength and clarity of his lectures, discourses whose perfect form masks the deep knowledge of books and of men out of which they are a distillation. As a teacher and as a writer, he has shown not only a truly impressive erudition and the rarest judgment and foresight, but also a devotion to his calling, a force of character, and a depth of conviction rare among teachers of this generation.

He early saw that a pacificism which refused to recognize dangers was as menacing to our civilization as the open espousal of evil. As Chaucer said of his parson, Jaszi has been to his students, "a shepherde and naught a mercenarie." His is the prophetic voice of an older Oberlin; with the accent of a foreign tongue, he speaks the language of King, of Bosworth, and of Fullerton. To know this great exile, helps one to understand a Dante, a Kossuth, or a Mazzini. During the heavy years since 1933, Oscar Jaszi has stood to his intimate friends and to many of his students like "the shadow of a great rock in a weary land."

Frederick B. Artz, '16

* * *

Dr. Jaszi received his Ph.D. degree from the University of Budapest in 1896. In addition to teaching at the University of Kolozsvar and at the

Continued on page 19

Dr. Phillip Sherman

Professor Phillip D. Sherman, one of the veteran members of the Oberlin College faculty in years of service, retires this year after 35 years of teaching in the English department.

Dr. Sherman has decided to retire this August in order to have more time for travel and research essential to completing his critical edition of Thoreau's "Walden." He will also have greater opportunity for creative writing in the fields of the critical and the bibliographical essay.

Preparation of an annotated bibliography of his library, preparatory to transferring it to an eastern university, is another piece of work he will undertake soon. Dr. Sherman's library, which includes many rare books and original manuscripts, is known among scholars all over the country. The university to which it is to be given will use the books and the literary manuscripts for research and publication.

Dr. Sherman had requested permission from the college board of trustees to retire three years before the automatic conclusion of his term of service. The trustees granted the request at their meeting May 25th.

Dr. Sherman, a graduate of Brown University in 1902, has been a member of the Oberlin College faculty since 1907, and professor since 1924. He received his M.A. degree from Brown in 1903. Last year Parsons College conferred on him the Litt.D. degree.

The success of "Illumination Night" on the college campus, considered by generations of Oberlin graduates to be the high point of commencement celebrations, has always depended in large measure upon Dr. Sherman, who each year since the custom was started in 1907 superintended the hanging of thousands of Japanese lanterns in Tappan square. *Oberlin* NEWS-TRIBUNE.

WITH THE FACULTY

**Trustees Accept
Sherman Resignation**

Members of the Board of Trustees announced the retirement of Professor P. D. Sherman of the English department following their meeting May 25. Professor Sherman is retiring this summer at his own request to engage in literary pursuits.

Vincent S. Hart, assistant investment executive of the College, was named investment executive on the staff of the treasurer, after it was voted to combine the offices of treasurer and investment executive under the direction of Treasurer William P. Davis.

Three new appointments to the faculty were made: Dr. Donald F. Brown, who has taught at the U. S. Naval Academy, was named instructor in romance languages; Leonard Diehl, director of athletics at the St. Charles, Illinois High School, was named instructor in physical education; and Mrs. Faith Fitch Hill, '33' of the Bureau of Educational Research in Science, Teachers College, Columbia, was named instructor in physics.

**Visiting Carnegie Professor
Appointed to Oberlin**

Prince Hubertus Loewenstein, authority on the contemporary history of central Europe, has been appointed visiting Carnegie Professor to Oberlin College to be on campus for lectures and consultation from February 23 through March 26, 1943. His appointment is made possible through the Carnegie Endowment for International Peace and was suggested to Oberlin by Dr. Nicholas Murray Butler, president of the Carnegie Endowment. Educated in Germany, Prince Hubertus Loewenstein was prominent in political affairs before he left his country in April, 1933. Since then he has devoted himself to writing. He is the founder and secretary-general of the American Guild for German Cultural Freedom.

**Dr. Harry N. Holmes
Appointed Consultant**

Dr. Harry N. Holmes, head of the department of chemistry and president of the American Chemical Society, has been appointed a consultant to the Chemistry Division of the National Defense Research Council. The appointment will require occasional trips to Washington.

Since his five-weeks lecture tour early in the spring through the west, Dr. Holmes has addressed chemists in Elizabeth, New Jersey, Akron, Chicago, and Pittsburgh, and on May 22 presented the Willard Gibbs Medal at Chicago to Dr. Thomas Midgley to whom the world owes ethyl gas. As president of the American Chemical Society Dr. Holmes presided at the national convention at Memphis, April 20. The membership now numbers 31,000.

On May 19 Dr. Holmes was summoned to Washington to a hearing by a committee headed by The Honorable Maury Maverick, acting at the request of Donald Nelson. On June 12 Dr. Holmes delivered the Commencement Address at Lakewood High School. The exercises were held in the Music Hall of the Cleveland Public Auditorium.

**Fisher Joins Army
Air Corps in May**

Professor Raymond Fisher of the education department, left early in May for Miami, Florida, for preliminary training with the Army Air Corps. He will have the rank of captain. After the preliminary training he expected to be assigned to Maxwell Field, Alabama, where he was to give educational tests to army pilots. Professor Fisher had officer's training in the last war.

He is the second member of the Oberlin faculty to join the armed forces. The first was Robert Gunderson, member of the speech department, who was called into the army last summer.

Nathan Dane II, instructor in classics, was the third faculty member to be called by the army. He left May 20 to join a medical detachment at Camp Bowie, Texas.

**Sally Marsh and Robert
Wagner Engaged**

The engagement of Sally Isabelle Marsh to Dr. Robert Wagner was announced in May. Miss Marsh is secretary to Dean Wittke, and Dr. Wagner is instructor in the mathematics department. No date has been set for the wedding.

Faculty Notes

Dr. R. P. Jameson, head of the department of romance languages, addressed the Modern Language Teacher's Institute held at Ohio State University, June 15-20, under the auspices of the Ohio Modern Language Teachers Association. Dr. Jameson lectured on "Linguistic Aspects of Foreign Language Teaching," and "France and French Culture in the Classroom." In May Dr. Jameson was in Philadelphia to attend the spring meeting of the Council of the American Association of University Professors . . Professor H. H. Thornton of the department of romance languages spoke at the College Club in Cleveland, April 28, before the Italian Literary Club of Cleveland on the subject, "Giuseppe Baretti in England" . . .

Professor Herbert G. May of the Graduate School of Theology was elected moderator of the Medina Association of Congregational-Christian Churches at the semi-annual meeting held April 22 in the Litchfield Congregational Church . . . Dean T. W. Graham attended a meeting of the National Board of the Y.M.C.A. in Cleveland May 16 and 17 and preached in the Trinity Methodist Church in Cleveland on May 17. He delivered an address before the membership section of the Employed Officers Conference of the Y.M.C.A. in Cleveland May 20. On the following two days he spoke at the 100th anniversary of Congregational Christian Churches in Jackson, Michigan . . .

Professor Clarence T. Craig has contributed an essay on "The Problem of the Messiahship of Jesus" to the volume of New Testament Studies recently published by the Abingdon-Cokesbury Press. The studies were by former pupils of Professor Lowstuter of Boston University, and were presented to him as a testimonial on his recent retirement . . . Professor Walter M. Horton read a paper at a conference of the American Branch of Faith and Order in New York City late in May. .

Professor Daniel Harris of the Conservatory was a soloist May 13 in Bach's B Minor Mass at St. James Episcopal Church in Cleveland . . . Professor Harris, Professor Harold Haugh and Miss Helena Strassburger were guest soloists for the presentation of Hayden's "Creation" at the First Congregational Church of Elyria on May 19 . . . Professor Haugh was one of the soloists at the 10th annual Bach Festival given by the Baldwin-Wallace Conservatory of Music at Berea, Ohio, May 22 and 23 . . .

Professor Arthur L. Williams was in Savannah, Georgia, April 24 as guest conductor of the Georgia All-State Band, composed of 100 high school musicians. The band played before the Georgia Education Association . . . Professor Maurice Kessler attended the annual Bach Festival in Bethlehem, Pennsylvania, May 14 and 15 . . .

Dean Carl Wittke attended meetings of the Mississippi Valley Historical Convention at Lexington, Kentucky in May and talked before the trustees and faculty of the University of Louisville at Louisville, Kentucky . . . Dr. Wolfgang Stechow, professor of fine

Continued on page 24

UNDER THE ELMS

Summer Enrollment
Estimated at 486

Although final figures on summer enrollment were not available as this issue of the magazine went to press, previous estimates based on advance registration placed the number of students at 486 in the three major divisions of the College for the first eight weeks. The number for the second eight weeks was expected to be lower and in the neighborhood of four hundred.

New freshmen entering this term numbered 68. Ten of these were registered in the Conservatory. Of the 68, 58 were men. The Graduate School of Theology and Kenyon are working together on a joint summer session. Kenyon has sent 10 students, and two professors: Dr. Corwin Roach to teach the Old Testament, and Dr. William Seitz to teach missions.

Freshmen arrived for a brief orientation period on Saturday, June 6, and classes started June 8. Men's dormitories open for the summer are the Men's Building, Noah, Embassy, and the Quad; women's dormitories are Talcott and Baldwin; and dining halls are the Quad, Webster, Talcott, and Baldwin.

Jascha Heifetz Headlines
Artist Recital Series

Jascha Heifetz, world renowned violinist will return to Oberlin for the first time since 1934 when he appears on the Conservatory Artist Recital Series next December 1. The 1942-43 series includes ten concerts, three of them by the Cleveland Orchestra, conducted by Dr. Artur Rodzinski, on October 27, December 15 and March 9. Emanuel Feuermann, 'cellist, who was to have played on the series on November 10, died last month after the list had been made up. As yet, no one has been selected to take his place.

Other artists and the dates of their concerts are Povla Frijsh, mezzosoprano, November 3; Reginald Stewart, pianist, November 17; Claudio Arrau, pianist, January 11; the Gordon String Quartet, February 11 and 12; Charles Kullman, tenor, February 16.

All-American Rating
Goes to Review

All-American honor rating in the Associated Collegiate Press' judgment of college newspapers was given to the *Review* this year. The judgments were made on the type of school, enrollment and frequency of publication of the paper. Papers were scored on the basis of news stories, editing, features, and content and make-up in general. Editors of the *Review* this year were Norman Lyle, Jr., '42, of Birmingham, Michigan, who left school to enlist in the Army Air Corps, and Victor Stone, '42, of Maywood, Illinois, Lyle's successor.

Wagenet Wins
Mercer Prize Contest

The Mercer Prize in Economics was awarded this year to Gordon Wagenet, '42, of Washington, D. C. for his paper "The Relation of the Consumer to Certain Cash-Credit Agencies and their Control." The prize of $125 has been given annually for some years by Colonel Aaron L. Mercer, '11, of Cleveland. Usually two awards are made but there were no junior class participants this year.

Reverend Joseph King
Accepts First Church Call

The Reverend Mr. Joseph F. King, pastor of Plymouth Congregational Church of Lawrence, Kansas, has accepted the call of the First Church at Oberlin to become its pastor on September 1.

Dr. King is a graduate of Park College, Missouri in 1928 and received his Bachelor of Divinity degree from Chicago Theological Seminary in 1931. He did graduate work in Edinburgh and Berlin, receiving his Ph.D. degree. He was ordained to the ministry in 1933 and went that year to Lawrence, Kansas. At present he is moderator of the Congregational-Christian Churches of Kansas. He is the son-in-law of Dr. Albert W. Palmer of Chicago Theological Seminary.

Dr. King, who becomes the eighth pastor of Oberlin's oldest Church, succeeds the Reverend James Austin Richards, who resigned in January to accept a pastorate in Mount Dora, Florida.

Students Miss Goal
On War Relief Drive

The second consolidated War Relief Drive conducted by students this year bettered the first semester's total of $527 but fell considerably short of the $1500 goal set for local and national relief agencies. The total raised for the second semester was $834. Agencies benefiting included the Red Cross, United China War Relief, World Student Service Fund, Foster Parent's Plan, National Infantile Paralysis Fund, The Russian War Relief Drive, and the Phillis Wheatley Community Center.

Provide for Summer
Session Council

Student approval of an amendment to the constitution of the student council provides for a summer council to be composed of six officers. Members of the regular council remaining for the summer will retain their positions and vacancies were to be named by appointment of the regular council. Among the other organizations functioning during the summer will be the *Review* which will be issued on Fridays in a reduced size; the Oberlin Forum with Alan Gordon, '44, of Cleveland, as chairman; the *Yeoman* will put out a summer issue; the Y's which are combining for the summer; the O. D. A. which will give two plays this term, and the C. D.A. under the leadership of Winifred Bishop, '44' of Culver, Indiana. The Oberlin Consumers' Co-operative is opening for the summer term in a new first floor location at 23 South Main Street. The new manager is Kay Hardin, '42' of Evanston, Illinois who is replacing Jack Elliott, x'41, who has resigned because he is subject to the draft in the near future. The new Co-op president is Lloyd Swift, '43' of Wilmington, Delaware.

Faculty Contributes
Talent for War Relief

Faculty, students and townspeople combined to present a stage revue for the benefit of the British War Relief Fund in Warner Hall on May 2. A full house greeted the performers and contributed $500 for war relief. The faculty's main portion of the show was staged in the Cuckoo Club with Dr. Ralph Singleton, '23' as Master of Ceremonies. Miss Frances Nash directed the last part of the program which featured "The Gay Nineties in Song and Dance."

Students Organize
Victory Garden

One phase of the summer term recreational program planned by the student council includes a victory garden to be operated by the students in an area south of Noah Hall. Individuals may have their own plots or may work on a cooperative plan with equipment furnished by the department of buildings and grounds. Students plan to sell the produce and divide the profits according to the time spent by each worker. One group of students have been studying the possibility for part time work during the summer on near-by farms.

Announce Winners
For Class of 1915 Contest

John Rawlinson, '42' John Christie, '42' and Ralph Hirschmann, '43, the affirmative team, defeated the negative team of Robert Hahn, '42, Harry Otis, '42, and Howard Stanton, '43, in the Class of 1915 Prize Debate on the subject, "Should Congress Adopt the Keynes Plan of Compulsory Savings Taxation for the Duration of the War?" The winners received 50 dollars apiece. Rawlinson and Christie were also winners in the Class of 1915 Oratorical Contest in April, receiving 60 and 40 dollars respectively.

In the Class of 1915 Prize Essay Contest, Hunter Dupree, '42' took first place and Sheldon Wolin, '42' second, writing on the subject, "What Would Be the Probable Consequences of an Axis Victory, from the Point of View of the Political, Economic, and Moral Interests of the United States?" Victor Stone, '42' and Nathan Weiss, '42' took first and second places respectively on the subject, "The Future Role of Labor in the American Political System." First prizes on these two subjects were $75 and second prizes were $50.

Those elected to Delta Sigma Rho as announced at the prize debate were William Feicks, '42' Ralph Hirschmann, Harry Otis, Irving Phillips, '42' John Rawlinson, and Howard Stanton.

Faculty Approves
Discipline Plan

A new plan for revision of the Men's and Women's Boards calling for equal representation of students and faculty on disciplinary questions was approved by the faculty in May.

The Men's and Women's Boards will each consist of six faculty and six students with the dean of college men and the dean of women serving as ex-officio members of their respective boards. In addition there will be a joint disciplinary committee with equal faculty student representation, elected from the members of the Men's and Women's Boards with the dean of men and women serving as ex-officio members and as co-chairmen of the joint discipline committee.

Extend Use of Rec Hall
Facilities Next Near

The College prudential committee has approved a plan, worked out by the Student Council and the College recreation office, whereby Rec Hall, the campus recreation center in the Men's Building, will be open next year in addition to the present evening periods between the hours of 3:00 and 5:30 daily for student use of the bowling alleys, billiard tables and other facilities. Mrs. Helen R. Balcomb, hostess

at Goodrich House, will be in charge. The offices of the Y.M.C.A., the Y.W.C.A, the Hi-O-Hi will remain at Goodrich and the parlors will be used for meetings of various campus organizations with the permission of Mrs. Balcomb. Under this plan Goodrich will cease to function as a recreation center.

Five Upper Classmen
Selected as Counsellors

Selected by Dean Edward F. Bosworth as freshman counsellors for next year are Student Council President Elmer Engstrom, '43' from Oak Park, Illinois; Football Captain-Elect Robert Kelner, '43' from LaGrange, Ohio; and, three sophomores: William Diehl of York, Pennsylvania, William Hurley of Middletown, New York, and Sheldon Wolin of Buffalo, New York. These men will serve as counsellors in the Men's Building and in the smaller freshman men's dormitories on North Professor Street.

John Anderson Receives
1942 Gray Scholarship

John Neil Vincent Anderson, student at Central High School, Duluth, Minnesota, has accepted the Gray Scholarship award for 1942.

The scholarship, which pays full tuition for the full college course valued at $1200, is awarded annually. The scholarship was made possible by alumni and friends of Glen Carlton Gray, '11' one of Oberlin's greatest athletes, who was killed in a hunting accident in 1921. It is awarded on the basis of all-around ability.

Anderson has letters in basketball, football and track. He has been a class officer, belongs to the National Honor Society, and received the American Legion Award. He has been active in dramatics and the Hi-Y.

Anderson has been permitted to enter College late this fall in order that he may spend the summer as timekeeper, working on the construction of the Alaska-Canada highway under Mr. W. B. Matter, '14' of the Standard Salt and Cement Co., Highway Division.

Publications Code
Has One Major Change

The copy inspection ruling for the student publications reported in the last issue underwent one major change before approval by the faculty. The additional provision states "All contractual obligations between any editorial board and subscribers, printers, and advertisers must be fulfilled before salaries are paid." Otherwise the student plan for regulation of publications was accepted with minor revisions.

Lit Societies Sponsor
Vera M. Dean in Lecture

Culminating their year's activities the four women's literary societies joined together to bring Mrs. Vera Micheles Dean, director of the Foreign Policy Association Research Department to the campus for a lecture, May 5.

GEHRKENS (Contd.)

methods and the actual practice of music.

One of the most widely known men that ever taught in Oberlin, Dr. Gehrkens has been from the beginning of his career a leader in the Music Teachers National Association. He was the editor of their annual book of *Proceedings* for more than twenty years, and served as president. Long active in the councils of the Music Educators National Conference he was honored with its presidency. Dr. Gehrkens' "Questions and Answers" page is one of the features of *The Etude*. His ideals and principles of teaching have been presented personally to thousands of students here and in summer schools of various Universities, and through a host of books have in truth penetrated the whole world. After early works on *Terminology* and *Conducting* he began a series of texts filled with practical suggestions and wise counsel. Most recent of these is "The Teaching and Administration of Music in the High School" (1941) in which Peter Dykema shared. As Dr. Gehrkens like any successful pioneer has worked hard and long; he has been one of the chief builders of the greatest and most successful experiment in music education the world has known. He will be greatly missed but Oberlin can but join him in the hopes that these coming days may be as free and fruitful as those which he has long anticipated.

James H. Hall, '14

JASZI (Contd.)

University of Budapest where he held the rank of professor, Dr. Jaszi from 1898 to 1908 was an official in the State Department of Agriculture, and later served in Count Karolyi's post-war cabinet in Hungary as Minister of National Minorities. For 17 years he was editor of *Twentieth Century*, Hungarian Social Science Review.

Exiled from Hungary at the time of the Bela Kun uprising, Dr. Jaszi came to the United States in 1925 when he joined the Oberlin faculty. He is author and co-author of 13 different books and has contributed many articles to the *Nation, Foreign Affairs*, the *Yale Review, Slavonic Review, Social Research*, and *Public Opinion Quarterly*. He is the author of 13 articles in the *Encyclopedia of Social Sciences*.

OBERLIN FAMILY JOURNAL

Gulick, Griswold, Howard
Assist in War Effort

Dr. Luther Gulick, '14' trustee of Oberlin, was appointed on May 14 by Donald M. Nelson, WPB chief, to direct a permanent office of organizational planning, which will advise Mr. Nelson on administrative operations.

Another trustee, Dr. Erwin N. Griswold, '25' was to go to Washington on June 15, to assist Randolph Paul, tax advisor to the Secretary of the Treasury. Dr. Griswold will be working on new tax laws.

N. R. Howard, x'19, on leave as editor of the Cleveland *News*, who has been working in the Office of Censorship, has been advanced to assistant director of the Office of Censorship.

Dr. Gulick's new office as outlined by Mr. Nelson will study the operation of the various units of the WPB, examine relationships with other parts of the government devoted to the war effort, and will study methods of achieving decentralization in Washington and regional offices. Dr. Gulick has been working on supply organization problems for the War Department prior to this new appointment.

James Wickenden, '28,
Heads Tabor Academy

James W. Wickenden, '28' became headmaster of Tabor Academy, Marion, Massachusetts, on June 4. Wickenden comes to Tabor Academy after 12 years on the faculty of Deerfield Academy where he has been head of the biology department, has coached football, basketball and tennis and has worked with the glee club and band. After graduating from Oberlin he received his M.A. here in 1930. He attended the Salzburg, Austria, Music Festival in 1932, and has studied at the Marine Biological Laboratories at Wood's Hole, Massachusetts.

Establish Prize Fund
Honoring James McGill, '20

To honor the memory of the late James G. McGill, '20' the University of Rochester has a project to raise $2,000 for the "James G. McGill Prize" to be awarded annually to the senior student at the University, in the College for Men or the College for Women, "who has shown the greatest interest and achievement in government."

McGill was professor of government at the University of Rochester and former president of the Rochester Board of Education. He was the first chairman of the department of government at Rochester. He died March 4 in San Mateo, California.

Friends, associates, and former students are being asked to contribute to the fund of which Miss Isabel K. Wallace, vocational counselor of the College for Women of the University of Rochester, is chairman.

Aelioian Fellowship Goes
To Frances Brooks, '25

Frances Eleanor Brooks, '25' is the recipient of the Aelioian Fellowship of $1,000 for 1942-43. Miss Brooks is associate professor of English at Berea College. She has done graduate work

Frances Brooks, '25
... *Receives Aelioian Award*

both at Radcliffe College and Johns Hopkins. With the fellowship she plans to continue her study of English toward the Ph.D. degree.

Mrs. Barbara Smith Rae, '38' was named alternate for the fellowship. The fellowship is awarded by the College faculty committee on graduate study upon the recommendation of an advisory committee of Aelioian alumnae.

Percy J. Ebbott, '10, Heads
Reserve City Bankers

The banking magazine, *Finance*, for April 30, carries the following item about Percy J. Ebbott, '10'

"In selecting Percy J. Ebbott, one of the top-flight vice presidents of the Chase National Bank of New York, as its president, the Association of Reserve City Bankers could not have made a happier choice.

"He is regarded as one of the most capable and experienced commercial bankers in the country. Born at Fort Atkinson, Wisconsin, he started his career with the National Park Bank in New York. He is widely known, has a grand personality and is not only smart —but abuses the privilege.

"During the past few weeks, he moved up to the Fourth Floor at the Chase National Bank. This, in the eyes of bankers, is interpreted to mean that he is destined for a further raise in the banking world. 'Perce' is still young to hold such a high and responsible position.

"Prediction: He will acquit himself with distinction."

According to *Finance*, the Association of Reserve City Bankers is composed largely "of the top-flight policymaking bankers of the country."

Father, Son Serve
In Armed Forces

The first news of a father and son, both Oberlin graduates, serving in the armed forces was reported this past month. Sherwood Moran, '14' formerly at the Japan Mission of the American Board has enlisted in the Marines. He will have the rank of Captain. His son, also Sherwood Moran, '39' is a Yeoman in the Navy.

Another Brigadier General has come to light. He is Brigadier General George C. Reid of the United States Marines, stationed at San Bernito, California. He was enrolled in the Academy from 1894-96.

Oberlin's other Brigadier General James Roy N. Weaver, '06-'07' who was reported captured on Bataan, was awarded the Distinguished Service Cross in April.

Heads Nation's Largest
Congregational Church

The Reverend Dr. Alfred Grant Walton, '11, will become pastor on October 1 of the largest Congregational Church in the United States. Dr. Walton has been pastor of the Tompkins Avenue Church in Brooklyn. On May 27 the members of this church and the members of the Flatbush Avenue Church voted to merge with the consolidated church to be known as the Flatbush-Tompkins Congregational Church. Dr. Walton was invited to be the pastor of the combined churches which will be in the Flatbush edifice. The new church will have a membership of more than 4,100. The Tompkins Avenue Church which Dr. Walton has served has a membership of 2,337, and has been ranked as the third largest Congregational Church. Dr. Walton received his B.D. degree from Oberlin in 1914 and his D.D. degree in 1927.

Tufts Plays Organ
For Roosevelt, Churchill

William O. Tufts, Jr., Con. '34' had a unique experience on Christmas day, when as organist of the famous Foundry Methodist Church, Washington, D. C., he participated in the worship service attended by President Roosevelt and Prime Minister Churchill.

An account of Tuft's experiences appeared in *The Diapason* for March 1. In this he relates how secret service men were stationed all over the church, even inside the organ. Three days before Christmas Tufts went to the church to practice. He was escorted to the organ console by "a soldier fully armed even to fixed bayonet . . . My 'personal bodyguard' took his post beside the console and remained there the entire time I was at work and escorted me to the door when I left."

Tufts reported that the soldiers stationed in the organ chamber had to have protection for their ears. The full organ combination was too strong for them.

Robert A. Harper, '86'
Praised by Botanists

The *Bulletin* of the Torrey Botanical Club for May carries an account of the achievements of Robert Almer Harper, '86' emeritus-professor of botany at Columbia University. The Torrey Club which is 75 years old this year, congratulated Dr. Harper "on his eighty years of life" and called attention to the fact that for 29 years he was one of its most active members. He was president of the club from 1914-16 and served on many of its committees.

The report says of Dr. Harper: "The researches for which Professor Harper is best known are his classic studies in the morphology and cytology of the slime moulds and the ascomycetes. The beautiful figures with which his papers are illustrated have long served as models for later workers . . .

"His interests have never been confined to his own specialties; few men have had a broader knowledge of botany in all its phases. This is reflected in the thorough training of his students, many of whom have attained eminence. His keen and active mind earned the respect and admiration of those who worked under him and made him respected as a teacher."

Dr. Harper received his M.A. from Oberlin in 1891, and his Ph.D. from the University of Bonn in 1896. He taught at the University of Wisconsin before coming to Columbia in 1911 as Torrey Professor of Botany, a position he held until his retirement in 1930.

George Vradenburg, '10'
Praised for YM Work

More than 400 persons, including Ohio's Governor John W. Bricker, paid tribute to the work of George Vradenburg, '10' in developing the Toledo Y.M.C.A. at a dinner in Toledo, April 29.

Mr. Vradenburg retired this year as president of the Y.M.C.A. after serving in this capacity for 10 years. He has been a member of the board of directors of the Y.M.C.A. since 1918 and was reelected this year.

Among Vradenburg's achievements have been the establishment of Hi-Y Clubs in Toledo in 1917, the creation of the Y Men's Club, now an International Y.M.C.A. organization; leading the campaign for $1,500,000 to erect the Jefferson Avenue Y.M.C.A.; the opening of the Indiana branch; and, the expansion of the Y.M.C.A. Camp Storer, at Napoleon, Michigan.

A tribute in the form of a scroll written by Dr. Grove Patterson, '05' a member of the Y.M.C.A. Board for more than 40 years, was presented to Vradenburg at the banquet. Of Vradenburg's service to the Toledo youth, the Toledo *Blade* said editorially:

"Governor Bricker, in a notable address at the annual meeting of the Toledo Y.M.C.A. Wednesday evening, did not exaggerate when he said that George A. Vradenburg, retiring president, has built an enduring monument by his leadership in the work of character building among boys and young men. For 10 years Mr. Vradenburg has given the Association not only devoted and sacrificial direction but he has brought to the work the talents of an able businessman.

"Here is an institution which not only does its full duty, with a great program for youth, but it is an institution which is competently operated 'in the black.' This record is principally the product of the work of George Vradenburg over the past decade. Now that he is retiring from the presidency, Toledo men and women do well to make an expression of their appreciation for the splendid contribution to a better day which he has made."

Mary Meriwether, '70
Dies; Last Member of Class

The death of Mrs. Mary Robinson Meriwether, the last surviving member of the Class of 1870, brings to a close an era of old Washingtonians. For sixty-eight years she was a resident there, leaving nearly two years ago to live with her daughter, Mrs. E. B. Henderson, in Falls Church, Virginia, and later with another daughter, Mrs. T. G. Nutter, in Charleston, West Virginia, where she died, April 6. Funeral services were held in Washington, D. C., at the Fifteenth Street

Presbyterian Church of which she was one of the founders.

She was born in Alton, Illinois in 1848, the daughter of Sarah and Robert Jonathan Robinson. On account of better educational facilities, her father moved his family to Wellington, Ohio. In 1866, she entered Oberlin College and was graduated in 1870.

For two years she taught in Columbus, Ohio and in 1872 was appointed to the faculty of the first Negro high school in Washington where she taught until her marriage to James H. Meriwether, who practiced law in the District of Columbia.

For many years, Mrs. Meriwether was active in the religious, cultural, and civic life in Washington. Her chief interest was the development and maintenance of "The National Home for the Relief of Destitute Colored Women and Children," established by an Act of Congress in 1863. In 1880, Mrs. Meriwether, along with two other Negro women, was invited to join this organization. In this work, she was associated with such women as Mrs. Horace Mann, wife of the great educator, Mrs. S. C. Pomeroy, whose husband was one of the senators from Kansas, and Miss Swann, sister of Senator Morrell of Maine. Mrs. Meriwether was president until she left Washington.

In 1917, a movement was launched to take away this institution from those in authority. Mrs. Meriwether appeared before a United States Congressional Committee and the continued existence of this organization was due largely to her efforts.

As two of the founders of the Fifteenth Street Presbyterian Church, she and her husband served on nearly every committee, and one of the last acts of the pastor, the late Francis J. Grimke, was to write a letter to Mrs. Meriwether in which he expressed great admiration for her character.

When the Young Men's Christian Association was organized in Washington, she served as president of the Women's Auxiliary.

Soon after her affiliation with Alpha Kappa Alpha Sorority, she presented this organization with the table which was used in negotiating the establishment of Howard University and gave her consent to have the table presented to the University.

Mrs. Meriwether is survived by four children: Robert H. Meriwether, Mrs. E. B. Henderson, Mrs. T. G. Nutter and Mrs. E. Davidson Washington.

Furlough Book

Men on leave from the armed services who visit Oberlin are urged to sign the "Furlough Book" in the office of the president.

ATHLETICS

By Robert France, '43

With top honors going to the golf and track team for their Ohio Conference Championship victories, the Oberlin spring teams piled up the finest record in Yeomen history as they won 23 of 29 contests for a .793 percentage.

This year's Conference Championship in track must be accredited to the superb coaching ability of Dan Kinsey and the tireless efforts of the members of the team. Starting off with what looked like no more than a mediocre group, Kinsey and his men settled down to plenty of good hard work with their eye on the Conference crown. The final score found the Yeomen on top with 45½ points to runner-up Baldwin-Wallace's 36. Case placed third with 25. The victory marked Coach Kinsey's tenth in 14 years and Oberlin's fourteenth in the forty year history of the "Big-Six."

Co-captains Dave Hildner and Jack Orebaugh did a fine job of leading their teammates. Hildner copped a first in the pole vault for the third straight year and took a fourth in the broad jump, Orebaugh won the century dash, took a second in the 220, and came from behind to win in the mile relay.

Herb Hansen, number two man on the tennis squad, traded his racket for a pair of spiked shoes and took the 880 with plenty of room to spare. Senior Tom Wood tied for second in the pole vault, and Eaton Freeman, a junior, placed second in the mile.

After winning the triangular meet with Case and Baldwin-Wallace reported in the May issue the track team defeated Wooster 84-47, nosed out Bowling Green by one and a half points to retain the title in the North-western Ohio meet; won the triangular meet with Mt. Union and the MacDonald A. C., and defeated Ohio Wesleyan 73-58.

GOLF

Coach Hayden Boyers' golfers scored one of the most impressive victories in Ohio Conference annals when Dick Holmes, Captain Johnny Carlisle, and Bob Drummond, placed first, second, and third respectively for individual honors, and joined up with sophomore Don Becker to win the team championship by 35 strokes. This marked Oberlin's third triumph in seven years. Potentially a sub-par golfer, Holmes found himself in the Conference medal play to turn in a 39-37-38-42 for a 156 total that was 12 better than any competing school's individual score. Holmes' record goes into the field of phenomenal golf when the extremely bad weather is taken into consideration. The whole match was played in a steady downpour of rain, and the fourth nine brought on a veritable cloudburst. Carlisle and Drummond pushed their teammate all the way to post 159 and 161 respectively. Sophomore Becker held up well under the trying weather and came in with a 184 total.

Previous to the Conference match the Yeomen had marked up the finest regular season's record in golf history winning five of six matches, the only loss being an 8½-7½ heartbreaker that went to Denison. Victories came over the Scots twice, Denison once, and Kenyon twice.

TENNIS

Coach Bob Keefe's varsity netters had little trouble in dual matches dupli-

Co-Captain Jack Orebaugh, Coach Dan Kinsey and Co-Captain Dave Hildner with the Ohio Conference championship track trophy. Right, Richard Holmes, Ohio Conference Golf Champion, who with the other members of the golf team was to enter the National Collegiate Athletic Association Golf Tournament at Notre Dame, June 21-27.

cating last season's record of eight straight. Five of the eight this season were shut-outs for the Yeomen. The closest dual match was with Kenyon who lost by a 4-3 score. Kenyon, however, made this up in the Conference play.

Contrary to earlier reports, the Kenyon tennis team entered the conference matches and proceeded to walk away with the honors as usual. Murray and Dalby of the Lords both reached the singles finals but decided to play off the match under more favorable weather conditions since cold and rain had forced the matches onto the asphalt courts. Kenyon's doubles combination of Murray and Burke had no trouble in taking the doubles title.

Oberlin's singles entries of Captain Dick LeFevre and Clint Doggett lasted to the semi-and quarter-finals respectively, and the doubles combine of LeFevre and Shel Wolin went to the semi-finals to give the Yeomen a third in team totals. Denison took second in team honors.

BASEBALL

This year's varsity nine took its worst beating from the weather man who rained and snowed them out of Continued on page 24

ALUMNI CLUBS

Two Meetings
In Chicago Area

The Oberlin Women's Clubs of Oak Park and Chicago held a joint meeting April 11 at the home of Mrs. Eone Goodenough Harger, '33' in Oak Park. The program opened with musical selections on the radio which, according to the announcer, were especially prepared for the Oberlin women of metropolitan Chicago.

Mrs. Edith Ballou Higgins, '10' summarized a dozen or more of the season's new books—both fiction and non-fiction—and then gave particular attention to "Cross Creek" people as realistically described by their neighbor, Marjorie Kinnan Rawlings.

* * *

The Oberlin Women's Club of Chicago held their last meeting of the year on May 9 at the home of Mrs. Catherine Smith Brown, '28' Mrs. Brown and Miss Florence Pope, '11' were co-hostesses. Mrs. Brown, who spent the past winter delving into modern Chinese history, read a paper on the "Soong Sisters" and extracts from Emily Hahn's book on the subject. A discussion followed.

Officers elected for 1942-43 were Mrs. Helen Templeton Young, '26' president; Mrs. Clara Clark Beggs, '19' first vice president; Mrs. Dorothy Bracken Pettijohn, '28, second vice president; Miss Jean Filkins, '38' treasurer; Mrs. Sara Meriam Shannon, '21-'22' recording secretary; Mrs. Laura Shurtleff Price, '93' corresponding secretary; Mrs. Elizabeth Wilkinson Hudgens, '40' membership chairman; and Mrs. Helen Waller Metcalf, '12' councillor to the Oberlin Alumni Association.

Stark County Group
Holds May Picnic

Miss Frances Cade, '34' executive-secretary of the Oberlin-Shansi Memorial Association, showed movies and spoke on the Oberlin schools in China at a picnic of the Stark County Oberlin Alumni Club, held at Silver Bear Park, Alliance, May 16. Twenty-two were present for the outing. Miss Eva Lee Sackett, '26' Alliance, brought a sextet from her school to sing for the group. The outing was arranged by Mr., '08' and Mrs. Howard B. Sohn. Mr. Edward Heald, '07' president of the club, presided.

Those attending were Mr. and Mrs. William Ailes (Louise Russell, x'99); Mr., '07' and Mrs. Edward Heald (Emily Ainsworth, '07); Mr., '08' and Mrs. Howard Sohn; Mr., '17' and Mrs. Robert Hartman (Freda Shinkle, '17);

Mrs. Helen Loomis Riley, '19; Miss Ruthanna Davis, '26; Miss Eva Lee Sackett, '26; Mrs. Elizabeth Sackett Barber, Con. '29; Miss Ruth Waltenbaugh, '30; Mr., '34' and Mrs. Robert Herbert (Jean Humphrey, '35); Miss Harriet Irwin, '37; and, Mrs. G. W. Irwin.

Harris, Love Visit
Pittsburgh Club

Pittsburgh's Oberlin Alumni Club welcomed two speakers at the annual dinner held at the Pittsburgh College Club, April 28. Donald M. Love, '16' secretary of the College spoke about the adjustments being made at Oberlin to meet the war emergency. Thomas E. Harris, '33' alumni secretary, made his first address since assuming his new work.

Officers for the coming year elected at the meeting were Mrs. Gertrude Schuchman Engstrom, '18' president; Mrs. Louise Wakeman Erler, '32' vice president; Mr. Elbert Shelton, '17' treasurer; Miss Barbara King, '41' secretary; and Mrs. Dorothy Hayford Watkins, '38' social chairman.

Attending the Pittsburgh meeting were Mrs. Cora Woodford Geegan, '96; Mrs. Nellie Moorhead Dougall, '99; Mr., '09' and Mrs. Victor Doerschuk; Mr. J. Chester Dalzell, '10; Mrs. Alice Peters Lawton, x'11; The Reverend Mr. Paul H. Elliott, '12; Mr., '12' and Mrs. Ray Booth; Miss Booth; Mrs. Ruth Anderegg Frost, '13; Mrs. Anne Collins King, x'14; Mr. and Mrs. J. Bard McCandless (Sarah Shuey, x'15); Mr., '17' and Mrs. Elbert M. Shelton (Carolyn Klinefelter, '18); Mr., '18' and Mrs. Ford E. Curtis; Mr. and Mrs. Birger Engstrom (Gertrude Schuchman, '18).

Mr., '21' and Mrs. Charles H. Adams (Muriel Easton, '22); Mr., '28' and Mrs. George B. Hatch (Virginia Bentzel, '35); Mr., '28' and Mrs. George M. Dougall; Miss Sylvia Geegan, '29; Miss Annis Dougall, '29; The Reverend and Mrs. Charles C. Berryhill (Katherine Demms, '29); Mr. Beryl Spicer Brandes, Con. '31; The Reverend, '32' and Mrs. Paul H. Erler (Louise Wakeman, '32); Miss Eleanor Graham, '38; Miss Margaret Jones, '38; Miss Katharine Frost, x'38; Miss Jane Stoltz, '38; Mrs. Dorothy Hayford Watkins, '38; Miss Virginia R. Norris, '40; Miss Barbara J. King, '41; and Mr., x'42, and Mrs. Rene E. Carroll (Eleanor Lenz, x'43).

The club was also happy to welcome the parents of two present Oberlin students: Mr. and Mrs. George Moore, parents of Peggy Moore, '43; and Mr.

and Mrs. Ira M. Smith, parents of Lily Marie Smith, '43'

Ellen Johnson, '33
Speaks in New York

The Oberlin Women's Club of greater New York held its annual spring luncheon meeting at the Midston House on May 16. Miss Ellen Johnson, '33' of the Oberlin Art Museum staff talked to the group and with the aid of slides reported on the growth and expansion of the Museum.

Mrs. Ruth Tracy Millard, '28' president, announced the award of the scholarship fund again to Joan LeCompte, Con. '43' Officers elected for the coming year were Mrs. Alice Kershner Gurney, '28' president; Miss Elizabeth Foley, '29' vice president; Miss Phoebe K. Eaton, '37' secretary; and, Mrs. J. Crawford Cartlin, treasurer.

Those attending the meeting were Mrs. Mary Miller Burnett, Acad. '97-'07'; Mrs. Caroline Kelso Russell, '93; Miss Helen T. French, '98; Miss Clara V. Jones, '04; Mrs. Edith Robbins Strong, '08; Miss Mabel C. Eldred, '09; Mrs. Ann Stewart Stowell, K '12; Miss E. Rosalie Raymond, x'13; Mrs. Ethel Ackley Noble, Con. '13; Mrs. Marjory Leadingham Miller, x '14; Mrs. Gertrude Roberts Rugh, x'14; Miss Marion M. Root, '17; Mrs. Gertrude Williams Moll, '18'

Mrs. Flora Mugge Campazzi, x'21; Dr. Margaret Dann, '23; Miss Edith M. Carson, '23; Mrs. Marion Downing Andrews, '23; Miss Dorothy J. Cook, '25; Mrs. Geraldine Solomon Rickards, '25; Mrs. Luella Wilson Vaile, Con. '27; Mrs. Virginia Tuxill Kyle, '28; Mrs. Alice Kershner Gurney, '28; Mrs. Ruth Tracy Millard, '28; Miss Elizabeth R. Foley, '29; Faith Peirce, '29; Mrs. Kathryn Childs Cassidy, '29; Miss Carolyn C. Dann, '31; Miss Helen Fauver, '31; Miss Sarah H. Metcalf, '33; Mrs. Anne Marks Graham, '37; Miss Phoebe K. Eaton, '37; and Miss Nancy Goodrich, '41'

Edith Carpenter, '26
Heads Cleveland Women

Members of the Cleveland Oberlin Women's Club held their regular meeting May 12 at the home of Mrs. William J. Ellenberger, Con. '90-'92' when the officers for next year were elected.

They are Mrs. Edith Phypers Carpenter, '26' president; Mrs. Mildred Martin Christian, Con. '27' first vice president; Mrs. Ruth Cross Utley, '31' second vice president; Mrs. Katherine Harroun, '37' secretary; Miss Lucy Dyson, '40' treasurer; and, Miss Emma Kobb, '26' publicity chairman.

The club again has given their scholarship to Virginia Lane, Con. '44'

A partial list of those present were Mrs. Amelia Reed Osborn, '04; Mr., '15, and Mrs. Merritt Vickery (Laura

Root, '15); Mrs. Katherine Kieffer Steinhilber, K '17; Mr., '27' and Mrs. Charles W. Lawrence (Helen Defenbacher, '27); Mrs. Margaret Badgers Mapes, '20; Mrs. Carol Wallace Clark, '20; Mrs. Alice Lockwood Andrews, '21; Mrs. Helen Long Fowerbaugh, '23; Mrs. Charlotte Guthrie Ewing, '25; Mrs. Gertrude Bell Merkling, '25; Mrs. Frances Littell Ewing, '25'

Mrs. Edith Phypers Carpenter, '26; Mrs. Mildred Martin Christian, Con. '27; Mrs. Mary McCallum Pearce, '27; Mrs. Lois McCaw Denton, Con. '28; Mrs. Cornelia Brookhart Stockstill, Con. '29; Mrs. Barbara Neikirk Long, '29; Mrs. Marjorie Richards Ashe, Con. '29; Mrs. Bertha Noble Cairns, '30; Mrs. Margaret Reed Gillette, Con. '30; Mrs. Ruth Avery Johnson, x'31; Miss Esther F. Schmidt, '35; Miss Harriet Irwin, '37; and Miss Mildred Zuck, '40'

Columbus Alumni Hear President Wilkins

Fifty-one alumni and friends of the Columbus Alumni Club heard President Wilkins speak on "Adapting Oberlin to the War and the Future" at a dinner meeting held April 27 at the Faculty Club on the Ohio State University campus. A brief business meeting followed during which Sydney Fisher, '28' was reelected president of the Columbus Club.

Those attending were Dr. Howard Russell, '87; Mr., x'94, and Mrs. Roy Williams (Verna Lockwood, x'97); Mr., '97' and Mrs. H. C. Marshall (Julia Jones, x'oo); Miss M. Edith Jones, Con. '99; Mr., '06' and Mrs. John G. Olmstead (Louise H. Olmstead, M.A. '31); Mrs. Clara Snell Wolfe, '09; Dr., '10' and Mrs. Fred O. Anderegg (Lenore McNish, Con. x'30); Mrs. Alice Fairchild Reynolds, '12; Mr. and Mrs. Sam Cobb (Charlotte Caton, '12); Mrs. Edith Higby Rey, '12; Mrs. Helen Laylin Hendrickson, Con. x'14 Mr., '18' and Mrs. Harvey Cheney; Mrs. Marion Dickson Cowell, Con. x'18; The Reverend Mr. and Mrs. Ross Miller (Beatrice Beal, '19); Miss Margrett Schultz, '19; Mr. J. H. Vermilya, '22; Mr., '24' and Mrs. James Liggett (Elizabeth Storer, '24); Mr., '25' and Mrs. Robert Williams (Dorotha Young, '27); Mrs. Stella Zieg Montgomery, '25; Mr. Sydney Fisher, '28; Mr. John Louis, '29; Mrs. Evelyn Simmons Good, '30; Miss Dorothy E. Niehus, '32; Mrs. Martha Woodmancy Derau, '32; Mrs. Dorothy Creel Donnelly, Con. '33; Dr. Ellsworth McSweeney, '34'

Mr. Sam D. Koonce, '36; Mr. John Moore, '36; Mr. John F. Tillotson, '37; The Reverend Mr. Oscar Nichols, T '38; Mr. David L. Cramer, '38; Mr., '39' and Mrs. Kenyon Cramer (Marion McClelland, '40); Mr. Willard Bidwell,

'40; Mr., '40' and Mrs. George Hammon, Jr.; Mr., '40' and Mrs. Winfield Smith (Margaret Nichol, '40); Miss Harriet Adair, '41; and Mrs. Julia Reed.

Ithaca Club Reports November Meeting

On the "better late than never" principle the Ithaca Alumni Club has reported this past month a meeting held last November at the home of Professor, '11' and Mrs. Robert Cushman (Clarissa Fairchild, '11). Between 45 and 50 people attended the buffet supper and the informal program that followed. Officers elected for 1942 were Mrs. Katherine Daugherty Garrett, '03' president; and Mrs. Margaret McCord Nixon, '39' secretary.

BOOK SHELF (Cont.)

observation and study . . . it is a basic treatise dealing with the geography, history, peoples, politics, economic life, and the international and cultural relations of the twenty countries of Latin America." Dr. Schurz has lectured widely, worked for commercial firms in Latin American trade, made a rubber survey of the Amazon Valley, was economic advisor to Government of Cuba, and has served the United States Government in many capacities including five years as chief of training, Social Security Board.

FACULTY (Cont.)

arts, has been appointed visiting professor at the German School at Middlebury College this summer. Dr. Stechow will be in Middlebury from July 6 to August 20 where he will give a special lecture series under the Henry Janssen Foundation. The series will be on the subject, "Hausmusik" from Bach to Brahms . . .

Professor Clarence Ward and President Wilkins have been appointed to serve on the new advisory council program instituted at Princeton University.

Dr. Ben W. Lewis, now on leave from the economics department, has had the job of organizing a price ceiling administration for Ohio, Indiana, Kentucky, and Michigan. He came to Cleveland April 30 to get the organization in operation . . .

Professor and Mrs. Birdsey Renshaw have a son, born May 23. Professor Renshaw joined the zoology department this year.

ATHLETICS (Cont.)

three scheduled games. Coach Throner's diamondmen still turned in a .500 season with victories over DePauw, Wooster, Muskingum, Kenyon, and Otterbein, and defeats at the hands of Bowling Green, Wooster, Otterbein, Ohio State, and DePauw.

Spring sports captains elected for 1943 include Paul Nelson, '43' of Norwood, New York, track; Clinton Doggett, '43' of Haddonfield, New Jersey, tennis; Robert Drummond, '43' of Oneida, New York, golf; and, Russ Spicer, '44' of Maplewood, New Jersey, baseball.

Special spring sports awards were made as follows: the Robert Reischauer Tennis Trophy to Captain Dick LeFevre; the J. D. Barnes Track Trophy to Jack Orebaugh, co-captain of track, who won this trophy two years ago; and the A. G. Comings Batting Trophy to Captain Paul Nawrocki, who averaged .350 this season.

Big Six Permits Freshman Play; Oberlin Adopts Rule

The Ohio Athletic Conference, meeting in Oberlin May 15, adopted a recommendation of the Ohio Conference Managers Association permitting freshmen to play on varsity teams. As passed the recommendation "favors the retention of the one-year residence rule for freshmen in the present emergency, but grants the permission of the member Conference schools to use freshmen, if they so desire, during the emergency."

The Oberlin faculty to set forth Oberlin's stand on the question passed the following recommendation made by the committee on athletics: "That participation in intercollegiate athletics may be allowed to a student during his first term of enrollment, provided such participation meets the continuing approval of his department head (Dean of the College or the Director of the Conservatory). After the first term, all men are eligible to participate in intercollegiate athletics providing they meet the general eligibility requirements. This recommendation is for the duration of the war or until otherwise changed."

The adoption of this regulation by Oberlin is in keeping with the war emergency program. It is considered important that as many men as possible receive the more vigorous physical training of intercollegiate sports, and on the accelerated program, a student would not have more than two and two-thirds years of participation. It is believed that some men will adjust more quickly to college life if they can enjoy the varsity sports competition, yet the deans have a constant check on each first term man, and can force immediate withdrawal from varsity teams, if the student's work is being impaired. Originally the freshman rule was in force to prevent the so-called "tramp athlete" or professional athlete from entering college to play football. This is inconceivable at such colleges as Oberlin, Swarthmore, John Hopkins, and at most colleges in time of war.

FIRST CHURCH...100 YEARS OLD

The 100th anniversary of the laying of the cornerstone of First Church, Oberlin's oldest public building and scene of many stirring events some of national interest, was observed in June.

Special recognition of the event was made at the services Sunday morning June 14, at which the Reverend Mr. Nicholas Van der Pyl, former pastor, preached, and at a centenary dinner Wednesday evening, June 17, the date the cornerstone was laid, at which Mayor Charles R. Comings, '90-'98' the Reverend Mr. H. B. Williams of the Methodist Church and President Wilkins extended greetings. Professor Clarence Ward talked on the architecture and Professor James Hall, '14' on the music of First Church.

For many years First Church was known as "The Meeting House," so varied were the activities that went on under its roof. It has served as a common school, a place for the showing of panoramic paintings before the days of the movie, and an auditorium for musical events, lectures and political rallies. It was Oberlin's first fire station with the hand operated fire-engine being kept in the basement. Thousands of Oberlin High School students have received their diplomas at graduation exercises there and from 1843 until 1908 the College Commencements were held there.

The First Church was the place of welcome for the Wellington Rescuers after their release from the Cuyahoga County Jail in 1859, and the Anti-Saloon League got its start there in 1893.

There were 62 charter members when the First Church was formally organized in 1834. Prior to the erection of Oberlin Hall religious services were held in the log cabin of Peter Pindar Pease. The congregation outgrew these two buildings and a room seating 800 in Colonial Hall served for a time. With the coming of Mr. Finney to Oberlin even this was not large enough. When weather permitted services were held in "The Tent" which Mr. Finney used in his evangelistic campaigns. It was at his suggestion in February 1841 that a church be built.

The plans for First Church were copied after the Broadway Tabernacle in New York with some modifications. A Boston architect drew the plans which were freely revised by members of the congregation. Inasmuch as a considerable portion of the labor was done by the congregation, it was fortunate that Deacon Turner, a member of the construction committee, was an experienced builder. It has been estimated that the cost of the structure was $12,000, but only a small portion of this was given in cash. Materials as well as labor were contributed in Oberlin and from friends elsewhere. Professor Robert S. Fletcher, '20' for example, has found in his research acknowledgements of "a hat, a cheese, four bushels of apples, a barrel of flour, a one horse wagon, and two cows from residents of Medina."

It took four years to complete the building which at the time was one of the largest auditoriums in this section of the country. The building was never formally dedicated.

For 23 years it was the only Church in Oberlin. Gone now are the horse sheds, the iron stoves and other distinguishing marks of the early period. The First Church has twice been renovated, in 1908 and 1927. It is the only major building of pioneer Oberlin which survives.

Much of the history of First Church has been assembled by Professor Fletcher. A special souvenir bulletin on the history of First Church was prepared for the occasion by Miss Florence Fitch, '97' Professor John Kurtz headed the Centennial Committee.

AMONG THE ALUMNI

By Lois Catherine Shelton, '41

ACADEMY

Men in Service
Maj. Thomas B. Prottman.

Arthur Allen Ward, '94-'95 died on February 8 at the Florida Sanatorium in Orlando, Florida. He was born at Odon, Indiana, on July 15, 1874, and after leaving the Oberlin Academy studied at Western (now Coe) College and at Yale University. His missionary work in Africa, India, and Ceylon covered a wide range: Y.M.C.A., church, teaching, industry, and administration. Besides acting as treasurer of the Ceylon Mission and of the Jaffna Council of South India United Church, he started several cooperative credit societies, was president of a cooperative bank, and manager of a printing establishment, book shop, and carpenter shop. He is survived by his wife, who is the daughter of President Bookwalter of Western College, and two sons.

1880
Mrs. Ella Johnston Goodrich died at the age of 86 on May 22, her birthday, in St. Petersburg, Florida, where she had lived for the past 20 years. She was the widow of E. J. Goodrich, who was on the Prudential Committee of the College from 1874 to 1903 and a member of the Board of Trustees from 1878 to 1912. Mr. Goodrich kept a bookstore in Oberlin for many years, and Goodrich House, on Elm Street, was their home. Mrs. Goodrich is survived by a son, Robert, of Wilmington, Delaware.

1884
Mrs. Mary Church Terrell, of Washington, D. C., is one of the prominent people whose biographies appear in the June issue of Current Biography. She was selected for this honor because "very few Negro women have approached the accomplishments of Mary Church Terrell in education, literature, and social service." Current Biography reports that "as the only girl in a Greek class with 40 boys, she recalls with pride being called upon to read and translate when Matthew Arnold was visiting the college."

1887
Mrs. Georgiana Mead Clarke and Miss Edith M. Clarke, '91' have returned to their home in Oberlin after spending the winter months in St. Petersburg, Florida.

1888
Mrs. Joe Beatty Burtt (Anna Gurney) has moved from Hart, Michigan, to 1570 Morada Place, Altadena, California.

1890 — Class Correspondent: Mrs. Ella M. Gibbons, 1010 Parkside Drive, Lakewood, Ohio.

In the report of the University of California on "Gifts Received" in the period between March 11, 1941, and March 6, 1942, the following books, given to the General Library of the University by Professor and Mrs. Charles A. Kofoid (Carrie Winter) of Berkeley, California, are noted: "Two hundred and seventy-four volumes of incunabula, principally in the field of the classics, 200 volumes of theology, 450 volumes on sport, 1200 volumes of travel, 5317 volumes in the fields of geography, general description and history, relating to Europe, Asia, Africa, the Near East, the United States, the Polar region, and Oceania, 100 volumes on ships and the sea. This material is supplementary to the biological collections assembled by Professor Kofoid over many years, and now housed in the Biology Library."

Miss Lillie Ann Lee, of Jersey City, New Jersey, writes that she has been teaching ever since leaving college, at first as an academic teacher, and since 1890 as a music teacher. She holds a high school rating, and now teaches in a W.P.A. night school. She closes with best wishes to the members of '90'

Miss Clara Louise Smithe of St. Petersburg, Florida, writes, "Outwardly life here in Florida seems to move along without great change" and quotes a friend as saying that "California is a tonic, Florida a sedative." "But the high spot for me this year was the opportunity to hear Dr. Frank Laubach from the Philippines."

Mrs. Henry M. Rood (Grace Mellen) writes from Claremont, California, where she is spending a year with her two older sisters. They were joined recently for a month by another sister, Mrs. James McCord (Margaret Mellen, '93), and the four of them enjoyed the colony of Oberlinites at Claremont. On her way west Mrs. Rood visited her daughter Margaret, who is the wife of a Methodist minister in Junaluska, North Carolina, and she reports that another daughter is head of a small hospital in connection with the Pine Mountain School in Kentucky. Mrs. Rood is raising a victory garden in California, which she says, "helps to ease the pain of separation from her beloved New England."

Mr. and Mrs. John Winter Thompson, Con., spend their winters in St. Charles, Illinois, and their summers near Charlevoix, Michigan. Mr. Thompson retired in 1938 after 48 years of teaching organ and theory at Knox College. He has published 60 compositions, which include 31 anthems, 20 organ pieces, and a number of piano pieces. He has also written several textbooks on harmony and counterpoint. His leisure time is now spent in writing, golfing, and fishing.

Miss Grace Harrison, whose life has been spent alternately between invalidism and semi-invalidism, reports that she is now enjoying much better health, and is able to "do more" and "go more" and work in her garden more than for a long time. Her address is 678 South Kingsley Drive, Los Angeles, California.

Dr. Roy Sexton is still at Sterling, Illinois, and hopes to do his part "for the duration."

Give to the War Scholarships Through the Alumni Fund

1891 — Class Correspondent: Mrs. Minnie Beard Siddall, 329 Elm St., Oberlin, Ohio.

Frederick William Mueller, Con., died in Minneapolis, Minnesota, on March 7. Mr. Mueller was born in Sandusky, Ohio, on September 8, 1863, and after his work at Oberlin graduated from the Leipzig Conservatory in 1896. During the years 1891-1902 he taught music at Knox College, with the exception of the year 1895-96, which was spent in Leipzig, Germany. From 1902 to 1913 he was director of the Conservatory of Tonkio College and from 1913 to 1915 he held a position as a travelling salesman, with residence in Oak Park,

Illinois. In 1915-16 he was director of the Northwestern Conservatory in Minneapolis, Minnesota, and after 1916 he taught in the McPhail School of Music in Minneapolis. His wife, Anna Elizabeth Forte, died in 1940. He is survived by three daughters and one son, Frederick W. Mueller, Jr., x'22.

1892 — Class Correspondent: Mrs. Agnes Warner Mastick, Bear Ridge Farm, Pleasantville, N. Y.

Miss Theodosia Healy Currier, daughter of the late Aaron H. Currier, and granddaughter of former Professor Albert H. Currier of the Theological Seminary, was married on April 2 at St. Petersburg, Florida, to Mr. James Miller Easter, II. Mr. Easter is connected with the Lincoln Electric Company and Mrs. Easter with the Halle Brothers Store in Cleveland. Their home is at 2431 Overlook Road, Cleveland Heights. Mr. x, and Mrs. Charles H. Ewing and Mr., '91' and Mrs. Seabury C. Mastick (Agnes Warner) were present at the wedding.

1893 — Class Correspondent: Mrs. Etta M. Wright, 189 West College Street, Oberlin, Ohio.

Mr. William E. Rodgers, Con., x, for many years a banker in Chagrin Falls, Ohio, died on February 24. In addition to his widow, he leaves a son and three daughters.

Dr. Junius L. Meriam, of Los Angeles, California, has finished work on his 300 page book, Activities, Projects, Units of Work, which is about to be published by the University of California Press. Fourteen hundred students have found and classified 8,833 curriculum units in the public schools for this book, which is a report of research study of the elementary school curricula in the United States. He planned to be at Yale University on June 9 to see his son, Lathrop, receive his Ph.D. degree.

Mrs. Clara Davis Bridgman returned in May to the home of her son, Brainerd, '31' in Durham, Connecticut, after being "on the road" since January 2. She was in Massachusetts during January and February and in New York and New Jersey during March. She then spent some time visiting Negro institutions in the south, which afforded her an opportunity to compare conditions there with the situation in South Africa. She reports the arrival last fall of her first grandchild, Margaret Kathleen, and also says that she has seen Mrs. Edward M. Blake (Mary Otis), of Chandler, Arizona, and Miss Florence Snell, of Northampton, Massachusetts.

1894 — Class Correspondent: Mrs. Louise H. Norton, Berlin Hts., Ohio.

Mrs. Miner G. Williams (Annie Abell, x) has a new address in Douglaston, New York. She now lives at 16 Prospect Street.

Miss Clara May, of Oberlin, who has spent the winter in Rockledge, Florida, is now visiting Mrs. Otis A. Brown (Esther Ward, '99) in Gatlinburg, Tennessee.

Mrs. Wells L. Griswold (Frances Fitch) on her way back from Florida spent several weeks at Boone Tavern, Berea, Kentucky, enjoying springtime in the mountains and meeting old friends. She is now at her home in Youngstown, Ohio.

Mrs. Louise Hill Norton is again at her home in Berlin Heights, Ohio, after an autumn visit with her daughter, Mrs. Ralph B. Noyce (Harriet Norton, '21) in Grinnell, Iowa, a winter in Rockledge, Florida, and a few days with friends in Berea, Kentucky.

1895 — Class Correspondent: Mr. C. Rexford Raymond, St. John Hotel, Charleston, S. C.

Mr., Con., and Mrs. Charles H. Adams (Margaret Jones, Con.), of Oberlin, had a recent visit with Dr., '96, and Mrs. Robert Cowley (Anna Parry, '97), who have retired and are now living in Berea, Kentucky.

The Reverend Mr. John A. Hawley, of Amherst, Massachusetts, is a part-time worker for the "Debt of Honor" Fund, which raises money for ministers' annuities. His son, Henry, '23, who has been head of the economics department at Hobart College, recently accepted a teaching position at Harvard University.

Robert F. Massa, of New York City, reports "a little war effort that may or may not finally count, and a moderately successful battle with the wolf at the door."

The Reverend Mr. Otto R. Newcomb since his wife's death two years ago, has been living with his daughter in East Lansing, Michigan. His son-in-law has been a chemist at the Michigan State College for 20 years, and his two sons are in government employ. One of his sons, who has been connected with the University of Michigan, is now reporting short wave propaganda. Although retired, Mr. Newcomb is actively interested in the Peoples Church, an interdenominational community church in East Lansing.

The Reverend Mr. William C. Prentiss, who has been pastor of the First Congregational Church at North Brookfield, Massachusetts, for the last 12 years, writes that his youngest son, Carlos, has fifty hours flying time to his credit and hopes to be in the United States Air Corps.

William H. Dawley, Jr., of Little Rock, Arkansas, has been busy re-organizing a P.T.A., which as a result now shows an increase in activities and membership.

Dr. Arthur S. Patterson, chairman of the romance language department at Syracuse University's College of Liberal Arts, and a faculty member for 43 years, has announced his retirement, effective in June. In addition to the B.A. degree from Oberlin, he holds an M.A. degree from Harvard, a Docteur d'Universite degree from the University of Grenoble, and a Diploma Superior from the Centro de Estudios Historicos in Madrid. Now an emeritus professor of romance languages, Dr. Patterson writes,

"Henceforth I'm free to come and go,
Spend winters where the flowers grow;
Then come back home, as robins do,
When spring returns and skies are blue."

The Reverend Mr. and Mrs. Ernest Partridge (Winona Graffam) still live in Valparaiso, Florida, where Mr. Partridge, besides being pastor of the Community Church, is giving a good deal of time to the chairmanship of the U.S.O. Management Committee of his county. He is also local registrar for the selective service registration, black-out warden, and deputy marshal of the village.

1896 — Class Correspondent: Mr. Fred P. Loomis, The Chimney Corner, 3401 Poppleton Ave., Omaha, Nebraska.

Dr. Arthur T. R. Cunningham writes from Honolulu, "I am basking in this glorious Hawaiian sunshine, taking life easy. Have very well recovered from my stroke, with no serious remaining effects."

1897 — Class Correspondent: Miss Ethelwyn Charles, 934 Park Ave., River Forest, Ill.

Dr. Alvan W. Sherrill, after an illness of three months, has recently resumed his practice. He serves on the medical staff of two hospitals and is teaching at the University of Pittsburgh Medical School in Pittsburgh, Pennsylvania.

Since his retirement from active business, Merrill A. Peacock has spent much time in travel. Mrs. Peacock died last August.

Miss Mary Louis Stranahan, of Litchfield, Ohio, died on March 28 in Medina, Ohio. She had been confined to her bed for the most part of the last three years.

1898 — Class Correspondent: Mr. Ira D. Shaw, 62 Walnut Street, Oberlin, Ohio.

Men in Service

Brig. Gen. George C. Reid.

Dr. Paul Prentice Boyd, Dean of the College of Arts and Sciences of the University of Kentucky, received the honorary degree of Doctor of Laws at the sixty-fourth annual commencement service of Park College, Parkville, Missouri, on May 25. Dr. Boyd was an instructor in mathematics and astronomy at Park College from 1899 to 1904, and received his Ph.D. from Cornell University in 1911. He became professor of mathematics at the University of Kentucky in 1912.

1899 — Class Correspondent: Mrs. Sarah Browne MacLennan, 181 Forest Street, Oberlin, Ohio.

According to word received in May by the American Board of Missions, Miss Annie Pinneo, head of the English department of the Orlinda Childs Pierce College for girls in Athens, Greece, was returning to the United States on the Drottningholm, a Swedish neutral ship then en route to Lisbon with Axis diplomats. Miss Pinneo, who was the representative in the Near East of the Women's Guild of the Eliot Congregational Church in Newton, Massachusetts, is the last of the American missionaries to leave Greece. She has studied at the Emerson College of Oratory, the Boston School of Social Workers, Brown University, and University of Washington. From 1909 to 1915 she taught in Izmir, Turkey, in 1916 she received full appointment as a career missionary under the American Board, and since 1922 she has been in Athens, Greece.

1900 — Class Correspondents: Miss Grace M. Charles, 934 Park Avenue, River Forest, Ill.; Mrs. Florence Heath Jameson, 126 S. Cedar Avenue, Oberlin, Ohio.

Dr. Carl S. Owen has been practicing medicine in National City, California, since completing his medical work at Northwestern University and his internship in Chicago. One of his sons, who is a dentist, and his son-in-law, a graduate of Annapolis, have both been made lieutenants, senior grade. Another son, his three daughters, and his seven grandchildren live nearby. Dr. Owen has been president of the High School Board since 1916, and Mrs. Owen has organized and now supervises a casualty station.

1901 — Class Correspondent: Mrs. Mary Savage Newton, 114 Moran Street, Oil City, Pa.

1902 — Class Correspondent: Mrs. Mary Stickel Brown, 51 Sparhawk, Amesbury, Mass.

Mr. and Mrs. James J. Jewett, of Riverton, Wyoming, recently entertained Mr. Jewett's granddaughter, aged six, while her mother was moving to Seattle, Washington. Her father, who is Mr. Jewett's son, is in naval service. Mr. Jewett reports that a daughter is a public health nurse at Cody, Montana.

Miss Florence Crocker teaches courses in world literature, American and English literature, and rhetoric at the La Salle-Peru-Oglesby Junior College, in La Salle, Illinois. This summer will be her seventh spent in Hollywood, California.

Mrs. Cornelius F. Keuzenkamp (Maude Porter), of Greenville, North Carolina, writes that "50% of the family income is going for war bonds," and that "life is strenuous, but no gray hair."

George A. Phillips, of Cleveland, Ohio, writes that his older son, George, is in the personnel department of the O.P.A. in Washington, and the younger, Johnny, is a lieutenant in naval aviation.

1903 — Class Correspondent: Mrs. Llewella Fessenden Heilman, 3218 Dale St., San Diego, Calif.

C. Jerome Jackman, of Minneapolis, Minnesota, is practising law and teaching in the University of Minnesota. He is a colonel in the O.R.C. and at the time of writing was awaiting call for active duty. His hobby is field artillery, and he says that he has "hopes and lots of spirit, class and otherwise."

1904 — Class Correspondent: Mr. Harry W. Bails, 812 Garfield Ave., Rockford, Ill.

Mrs. La Mira Trent Button, of Youngstown, Ohio, died on April 24 after a long illness. Mrs. Button was the widow of the late A. Lyman Button, '03, who was the executive secretary of the Mahoning Valley Industrial Council.

Miss Alma G. Stockey, professor of plant science and chairman of that department at Mount Holyoke College, retires this June with the rank of professor emeritus.

Miss Mary Hillis writes that she is doing her bit in Los Angeles, California.

Robert Paterson has for years conducted a hardware business on St. Clair Street in Cleveland, Ohio. He and Mrs. Paterson spent the winter travelling in the south.

Wreford Goss Chapple, son of Mrs. Lou W. Chapple (Marion Goss, x) and grandson of James R. Goss, Academy, x'68, is the hero the article "Take'r Down," by Cecil Brown in the May 16 issue of Collier's Magazine. Mr. Chapple, who graduated in 1930 from Annapolis as the president of his class, has been awarded the Navy Cross.

George C. Enders, of Defiance, Ohio, entered into voluntary retirement last June after 36 years of college teaching, 31 of which were at Defiance College. The occasion was marked by many expressions of appreciation, which included a letter from Governor Bricker, a newspaper editorial by Grove Patterson, '05, of the Toledo Blade, and several banquets in his honor. Defiance College conferred upon him the degree of doctor of literature. Dr. Enders is now the lesson writer of the Adult Bible Class Sunday School Quarterly for the Congregational Christian Churches, and does occasional lecturing and preaching.

1905 — Class Correspondents: Mrs. Ruth Savage Cross, 1114 West Forest Rd., Lakewood, Ohio; Mr. Dan B. Symons, 800 Elyrin Savings & Trust Bldg., Elyria, Ohio.

1906 — *Class Correspondents:* Mr. Roy Kinney, 728 Selma Blvd., Staunton, Va.; Mr. Emmett Thompson, 130 Woodland, Oberlin, Ohio.

Mr. and Mrs. *Emmett Thompson,* of Oberlin, moved on June 1 into their recently purchased home at 245 North Professor Street.

Mr. and Mrs. *Dean H. Lightner* (Grace Herreid, '08) have a new address in Mason City, Iowa. It is 11 Rock Glen.

1907 — *Class Correspondent:* Mrs. Ruth Johnson Boyers, 15 Oneida Ave., Mt. Vernon, Ohio.

Harold Rollin Rogers, oldest son of Mr. and Mrs. *Harold L. Rogers* (Helen Hall), was married on April 18 to Miss Ruth Fischer Kennedy, of Montclair, New Jersey.

Miss *Iris Haverstack* writes that she has moved to Canton, Ohio, in order to be nearer her work, and that she now lives at 300 18th Street, N. W. She plans to spend a good deal of her time in war emergency activities.

Professor and Mrs. *Edgar K. Stansfield* (Marilla Cooper), of Edmonton, Alberta, Canada, send news of their two boys. Their oldest son, Hugh, received his M.D. degree in March and is continuing for the army his research in blood transfusion at McGill University. David, a sub-lieutenant, was called into active service in the Royal Canadian Navy in December.

Louis U. Rowland, Con., director of music at Albion College, was granted the degree of doctor of music at the commencement ceremonies at Iowa Wesleyan College on June 8. Dr. Rowland is a member of the States Council of the Music Teachers National Association, chairman of the Music Departments of the Church Colleges of Michigan, and president of the Michigan Music Teachers Association. He has composed selections for solo voices, the organ, piano, violin, 'cello, and a cappella choir; he has written alma mater hymns for Oberlin College and Albion College. Dr. Rowland has appeared in concert as accompanist for George Hamlin, Lily Pons, Gustav Holmquist, and many other famous artists.

1908 — *Class Correspondents:* Mr. Arthur E. Bradley, 280 Oak St., Oberlin, Ohio; Mrs. Florence Pearl Goodenough, P. O. Box 294, Springfield, S. D.

Eugene C. Bird and his wife, a Wisconsin graduate, live in South Bend, Indiana, where "Birdie" is connected with Purdue University in cooperative extension work. They have two daughters, one of whom graduated from Purdue University, and the other from high school, this spring.

1909 — *Class Correspondents:* Mrs. Alice Blackmore Allen, 4037 Willys Parkway, Toledo, Ohio; Miss Ruth Johnston, 6041 Kenmore Ave., Chicago, Ill.

Men in Service

Lt. Col. George S. Woodard.

Lawrance Hart, x, writes that on May 1 he passed tests given by the Boston, Massachusetts, office for a commission in the ground forces of the Army Air Corps, and that this may prevent him from spending the summer in Mt. Tabor, New Jersey, as he and Mrs. Hart had planned. This winter he has been singing with the Apollo Club of Boston.

Miss *Rose Porter,* since 1936, has been general secretary of the Family Service Society of Salt Lake City, Utah. She is also the chairman of an area committee for the National Conference of Social Work, a member of the executive committee of the Salt Lake chapter of the American

Association of University Women, for which she is also chairman of the committee on social studies, and a member of the Utah State Defense Council.

Clement Hunt, of Camp Hill, Pennsylvania, is an air raid warden and a first-aider. He has two sons over 21.

Mrs. *T. M. Hyatt* (Cora Hunter), of Long Beach, California, writes that Mr. Hyatt is on duty in the harbor area, in charge of security, and their son, Bruce, who took his training at Northwestern University, is an ensign in the United States Naval Reserve and is awaiting the completion of his ship. Their daughter, Eleanor, is a nurse at Gorgas Hospital, in the Canal Zone. "That leaves Martha Jane, aged 15, and me a good deal alone," says Mrs. Hyatt, "but this is war!"

Judge *Ernest Van Fossan,* of Washington, writes that he has recently received a letter from Paul Griswold Huston, who taught '09 freshman English, and whom the class voted to make an honorary member. Professor Huston says, in part, "I have been teaching boys, altogether, since I left Oberlin. Somehow that has turned out to be my life work. I understand boys, like to live with them, and teach them, and, as with you, to hear from them from years back. If I have had any influence with boys, it is because I have given them my best, and have got them to read good books. Not long ago I had a reunion with one of my classmates at Princeton, and I told him what I now say to you, 'I am still 69 years young!' "

Mrs. *William A. Wheaton* (Gertrude Cody), of Cleveland Heights, Ohio, reports that her daughter, Eunice Cody Wheaton, who graduated this spring from the dramatic art department of Iowa University, is assisting in the work of a children's theater and does children's radio programs. Her son, William, is at Chicago University working on his Ph.D. in political science. Mrs. Wheaton devotes part of her extra time to speaking for China Relief, and during the past year she has sent in gifts from twenty organizations and churches.

D. Windsor Jones is general secretary of the Y.M.C.A. of Niagara Falls, New York.

The Reverend Mr. *Joel B. Hayden,* of Hudson, Ohio, recently spent a week in Washington, D. C. in conference with government officials concerning the youth problem and the place of private schools in the national picture. He writes that while there he had lunch one day with Judge Ernest Van Fossan and Dr. Raymond Gram Swing, honorary Litt.D., '40.

Miss *Florence Otis,* of Maywood, Illinois, has been asked to assist Dr. Lew Sarett, of the department of journalism of Northwestern University, during the summer session, as she did in 1936 and 1939. This year the annual of Proviso County High School was dedicated to Miss Otis, in recognition of her twenty years as a teacher of journalism in that school. Two editors of the *Oberlin Review,* Tom Boardman, '39, and Victor Stone, '42, have been trained by Miss Otis.

David H. Richert is a professor of mathematics and astronomy at Bethel College, North Newton, Kansas. He writes, "Our son, Roland, is instructor in the cavalry school, Fort Riley, Kansas, with the rank of lieutenant. Our daughter, Ethel, will be married this spring. Being alone in our home will be a great change for Mrs. Richert and me—and not a welcome one."

The Reverend Mr. *Earle Munger,* T, pastor of Plymouth Congregational Church in Waterloo, Iowa, represents the ministers of the city

on the Civilian Defense Committee and on the Waterloo Central Labor Union, and he also serves as chairman of the board of the new Waterloo Y.M.C.A.

1910 — *Class Correspondents:* Judge Lynn B. Griffith, Court House, Warren, Ohio; Miss Elizabeth Hughes, 6850 Crandon Ave., Chicago, Ill.

Men in Service

Brig. Gen. James R. N. Weaver.

Percy J. Ebbott is vice president of the Chase National Bank of New York, and was recently elected president of the Reserve City Bankers Association at their convention in Hershey, Pennsylvania. Mr. Ebbott is also director of the Nash Kelvinator Corporation of Detroit, Michigan, and of Allied Stores, Incorporated, of New York City. He has recently moved to 18 Pine Street, New York City. See Family Journal.

Dr. *Arnaud Marts,* president of Bucknell University, at Lewisburg, Pennsylvania, is at the head of the Pennsylvania state defense activities.

1911 — *Class Correspondents:* Mrs. Helen Wright Avery, Charlemont, Mass.; Miss Ethel Brubaker, The Fairfax, 43rd & Locust Sts., Philadelphia, Pa.

The Reverend Mr. *C. Burnell Olds,* T, formerly of Japan and now of New York City, was married on March 9 at St. Petersburg, Florida, to Mrs. Olivia D. Young, formerly of North China.

Mr. and Mrs. *Kenneth Rich* (Adena Miller) have recently moved to 4832 Dorchester Avenue, Chicago, Illinois.

Mr. and Mrs. *Robert Riggs* (Helen Morrison, '12), of Tulsa, Oklahoma, write that their oldest boy graduated from Dartmouth in May and entered the Naval Aviation Corps in June.

1912 — *Class Correspondents:* Miss Mabel J. Baker, 7338 Euclid Ave., Cleveland, Ohio; Mr. Raymond Booth, 834 Florida Ave., Mt. Lebanon, Pittsburgh, Pa.

Men in Service

Lt. Col. Russell A. Clark, Dr. Donald S. King, Lt. Com. Nelson Metcalf.*

Mrs. *Hoy Clayton* (Alice Abell) has recently moved to 3205 North Marietta Avenue, in Milwaukee, Wisconsin.

J. Hall Kellogg was elected moderator of the Cleveland Congregational Union on April 28. Besides being an active member of the Plymouth Church in Shaker Heights for a number of years, Mr. Kellogg is a member of the law firm of Hauxhurst, Inglis, Sharp and Cull, has served on the executive committee of the Cleveland Bar Association, is a member of Shaker Heights Board of Education, and has been a trustee of the Cleveland Congregational Union for four years.

Mrs. *George M. Bohler* (Ethel Rodimon) has moved from Princeton, New Jersey, to 514 Delaware Avenue, McComb, Mississippi.

The Reverend Dr. *Ralph Sockman* observed the twenty-fifth anniversary of his pastorate at Christ Church, Methodist, in New York City, in April. He has spent his entire ministry at this church, and the present edifice on Park Avenue was built under his leadership. Fo-fifteen years he has preached over a coast-to-coast radio network. Mrs. Sockman is the former Zellah Endly of Elyria, Ohio.

Mrs. *Alan D. Finlayson* (Anna Wendt), of

*Anyone knowing this person's full military address please send it to the Alumni Records Office, Oberlin College.

Cleveland, Ohio, sends no news about herself, but reports that *Mrs. Williams H. Dial* (Lilliann Blackwell), of Mt. Rainier, Maryland, has just completed a nine weeks' "brushing-up" course for nurses at the Garfield Hospital in Washington, D. C.

Mrs. Edward J. Lorenz (Alice Barber) has been on a year's leave of absence from the University of Toledo, taking graduate work in the field of marriage and family counseling at the Merrill-Palmer School in Detroit, Michigan. She has a son, Edward, who will be a sophomore in the fall at Oberlin, and a daughter who is finishing her last year of college preparatory work at Stephens College.

Carl E. Scofield for several years has been general secretary of the Y.M.C.A. in Winsted, Connecticut. He spent ten years of Y.M.C.A. work in India and China, and it was while in Nanking University studying Chinese that he met his wife, the former Dr. Elizabeth Kamphefner, of Los Angeles. They have two children, a boy and a girl.

Dr. Ernest Carroll Faust, of New Orleans, Louisiana, is in charge of the department of tropical medicine and the head of the division of parasitology at Tulane University. As consultant to the Secretary of War on tropical medicine, he spends one week every two months in Washington. Last summer he and his wife visited Brazil, Uruguay, and Argentina, and Dr. Faust lectured at the invitation of the medical faculty of Buenos Aires. He hopes to visit Mexico in July.

1913 — Class Correspondents: Mrs. Martha Nichols Blackwell, 1259 E. Erie Ave., Lorain, Ohio; Mrs. Frances Jeffery Jones, 53 Sagamore Terrace, Buffalo, N. Y.

Men in Service

Capt. Franklin P. Metcalf.

Mr., T, and Mrs. Royal Haigh Fisher (Josephine Wray), of Japan, are temporarily at 11 South Portland Avenue, Ventnor, New Jersey, but mail will always reach them c-o Mrs. H. N. Hoffman, 603 Hoffman Street, Elmira, New York. They have recently announced the engagement of their daughter, Miss Elizabeth Wray Fisher, to George Biro, '34' (See Class of 1934).

Mr. and Mrs. Earl W. Derr (Margaret Smith), of Rockford, Illinois, have a new granddaughter, Portia Williams, daughter of Mrs. George H. Williams (Marjorie Derr, '39), born on May 8 at Berkeley, California. Mrs. Derr has gone to Berkeley for a visit and expects to see *Mr. and Mrs. Russell Curtis* (Gertrude Edwards), and Miss Helen Treat while there. Mr. Derr is retreading tires under government restrictions.

Dr. Esther Crane, M.A., of Baltimore, Maryland, is head of the education and child development department of Goucher College. This year she has been meeting with other educational representatives once a week in New York City, studying the problem of "Education of Teachers for New Types of Secondary Schools."

Mr. J. Paul Munson is living on a farm in Groton, New York, just north of Ithaca, and is district superintendent of schools. He also does a good deal of work in connection with the sugar and gas rationing and the draft board.

Dr. L. Wendell Fifield, of Brooklyn, New York, is the minister of the Church of the Pilgrims, following in the footsteps of Henry Ward Beecher and Lyman Abbott.

Mrs. Lillian Jackson Sargent, of Los Angeles, California, is head of the music department in the Belmont Senior High School. She is also active in club work in Los Angeles.

Mrs. Randall M. Tuttle (Ruth Ewing), of Spencer, Iowa, writes that their two younger sons, Peter and Tom, both graduated from the chemical technology department of Iowa State College this spring.

Mr. and Mrs. H. L. Eckert (Lillian Chambers), of Hamden, New York, write that while they were in Albany, New York, in April they met *Mr. and Mrs. Harold N. Fowler* (Mary Blackford), of Washington, D. C., who were on their way to Gloucester, Massachusetts, where they plan to stay for six months and where Mrs. Fowler will work at her sculpture.

Mr. and Mrs. Frederick B. Peake (Mary Tower, '14), of Oak Park, Illinois, have a daughter, Mary, who will be a sophomore at Oberlin in the fall. Mr. Peake would like to locate a lost "round-robin" letter which circulated among *Jerome Davis, Robert Whitehead, LeRoy Griffith* and others for 25 years.

The Reverend Mr. J. Albert Hammond is pastor of Tory Hill Meeting House in Bar Mills, Maine. This church was made famous by Kate Douglas Wiggins' "The Old Peabody Pew." Mr. Hammond says, "All '13ers cordially welcome!"

Miss Minnie A. Tonts and *Dr. William T. Lawrence* were married at Craigmore, near Chikore, South Rhodesia, Africa, on February 13.

Miss Jean Louise Frost, a graduate with the class of '39 from Carnegie Tech in Pittsburgh and daughter of *Mrs. Leslie E. Frost* (Ruth Anderegg) is preparing herself for a career as a travelling reporter, as well as satisfying her love for adventure, by following a plan of working two years and then travelling for six or eight months. Accordingly, she has worked as a secretary in the Gulf Research Laboratory in Pittsburgh for two years, and has completed her first jaunt. Her trip took her to Laramie, Wyoming, where she enrolled in a five-weeks geology course given by the University of Wyoming, to Alaska on a 45 foot schooner, to Oregon where she spent some time on a ranch, and finally to Mexico. She is now back at work again, saving up for her next trip.

Franklin P. Metcalf, who for the past year has been a research associate at Harvard University, is now in officers' training school. He has recently been commissioned as a captain in the military intelligence section, primarily on account of his experience in China.

Gifts to the Alumni Fund Are Proper Deductions Under Income Tax Laws

1914 — Class Correspondents: Miss Lura E. Humlong, Genoa, Ohio; Mrs. Helen Work Scott, 650 Highland Ave., Rochester, N. Y.

Men in Service

Capt. Sherwood Moran.*

Robert Hickok, son of *Mr. and Mrs. Guy C. Hickok*, of Silvermine, Connecticut, was married on April 17 to Miss Evelyn Wight, in Dorchester, Massachusetts. Robert is associated with the United Press bureau in Washington, D. C.

Sherwood Moran has resigned from the American Board of Missions for the duration of the war and is now a captain in the United States Marines. He and Mrs. Moran (Ursul Reeves, '15) left Japan, on regular furlough, in July, 1940. Both of their sons are at the University of California. Donald is a junior in the department of mining engineering, and Sherwood, '39' is taking an intensive course in the Japanese language in preparation for a commission in the navy. The latter and his wife (Frances Anne Harvey, '39) are living in Berkeley. The Morans' youngest daughter, Barbara, enters college this fall.

Arthur P. Honess has finished his twenty-fifth year of teaching at Pennsylvania State College. He has been in charge of mineralogy in the School of Mineral Industries since 1931. His graduate studies were completed at Princeton University in 1934, and in October of that year he was married to Miss Ethel Wortley, of New York City. Their daughter, Mary Ann, is ten.

1915 — Class Correspondents: Mrs. Vesper Wood Davis, 249 Elm St., Oberlin, Ohio; Mrs. Margaret McRoberts Love, 12425 Fairhill Rd., Cleveland, Ohio; Miss Ella C. Parmenter, Solon, Ohio.

Men in Service

Mr. C. Weller DeGroff, Maj. James V. Polacek.

1916 — Class Correspondents: Mrs. Josephine Steinhoff Curtis, 189 W. College St., Oberlin, Ohio; Mrs. Esther Gearhart Bretz, Box 198, New Waterford, Ohio.

Dr. Reginald Bell, since May 4, has been a civilian consultant for the audio-visual aids agency of the Bureau of Aeronautics, Navy Department, Washington, D. C. This bureau has responsibility for consulting with all training officers in other Navy bureaus regarding the potential use, within their bureaus, of audio-visual techniques. Dr. Bell expects to be with this agency for a period of five months, after which time he will return to the school of education at Stanford University.

Mr. and Mrs. Albert Ludwig (Gladys Newman, '17) are living in Cheney, Washington, where Mr. Ludwig is a full professor and head of the department of social science and history at the East Washington College of Education. Their daughter, Lyndell, will be a sophomore in the fall at the University of Washington.

Miss Kathryn Bretz, daughter of *Mr. and Mrs. Edward R. Bretz* (Esther Gearhart), of New Waterford, Ohio, was capped on March 16 at the School of Nursing connected with St. Luke's Hospital in Cleveland, Ohio.

Mr. and Mrs. Bert H. McQueer (Leah Kirkwood) are still living in St. Mary's, Pennsylvania, where Mr. McQueer is employed by the Speer Carbon Company as a chemical engineer. Their elder son, Jack, graduates from high school this year and the younger, James, is now 13 years old. They picnic once a year at their camp in the hills with *Mrs. Vera Peterson Emery* of Brookville, Pennsylvania, and her family.

1917 — Class Correspondents: Mr. Francis E. Gray, 48 Arlington Rd., West Hartford, Conn.; Mrs. Hyacinthe Scott Baker, 4910 E. 6th Ave., Denver, Colo.

Men in Service

Dr. Paul B. Sheldon.

Mrs. Charles N. Kirk (Dorothy Birkmayr), of Toledo, Ohio is scheduled to give three addresses at the Finney Sesquicentennial Memorial, which is to be held in the Moody Memorial Church in Chicago, Illinois, from

*Anyone knowing this person's full military address please send it to the Alumni Records Office, Oberlin College.

June 21 to June 28. Her talks, which are to be given on June 25, 26, and 27, are on "The Ministry of the Spirit," "The Indwelling Spirit," and "Walking in the Spirit."

The Reverend Mr. Rudolf Hertz, of Eagle Butte, South Dakota, is superintendent of 27 Congregational Indian churches in and around South Dakota, and is also chairman of the school board and of the county chapter and local branch of the American Red Cross. He and his family usually spend the summer in a cabin in the Black Hills, but they plan to stay in Eagle Butte this summer.

Miss Erma Johnson, Con., writes that she spent the winter in Florida, playing with a trio. She is now teaching piano in Cleveland, Ohio.

Miss Edith M. Gates, of New York City, health education secretary on the national board of the Y.W.C.A., writes, "Since I have just completed a trip of rather unusual proportions and unique opportunities, I thought you might want to hear about it. In two months and three weeks I covered 10,933 miles in 24 states. I made 14 regular Y.W.C.A. visits ranging from Minneapolis, the northwest and California, Denver, Colorado, Topeka, Kansas, to Waterloo, Iowa, and Cincinnati, Ohio. At this point the invitation to speak at the closing session of the annual convention of the American Association of Health, Physical Education, and Recreation, stopped my homeward trip—for a 'side trip' from Cleveland to New Orleans. This convention was of value to me because of the consideration given to the joint responsibility of private and public agencies in the wartime program of physical fitness and recreation.... And I return to discover a New York University diploma arrived in my absence to report the completion of work for the M.A. degree, a period of study long delayed by so many jaunts into foreign lands in former years."

1918 — Class Correspondents: Mrs. Rena Bickerstaff Gove, 172 Elm St., Oberlin, Ohio; Mr. Harvey C. Cheney, 225 E. Pacemont Rd., Columbus, Ohio.

Men in Service

Dr. Donald D. Forward, Com. Nolon M. Kindell, Lt. Com. Luman H. Tenney.

Mrs. John M. Emde (Laura Hines) has recently moved from Hattiesburg, Mississippi, to 1210 Entaw Place, Baltimore, Maryland.

Mrs. Ernest W. Houlding (Florence Bickerstaff), of Berkeley, California, has been elected president of the California Association of Clinical Laboratories for 1942.

The marriage of Miss Janet Elmore Greene, daughter of Professor, Academy, '10-'14' and *Mrs. Theodore Meyer Greene* (Faith Nelson), of Princeton, New Jersey, to Ensign Harvey Horton Meeker, Jr., took place on May 2 in the Princeton University Chapel. Mrs. Meeker is the granddaughter of the Reverend Mr. Charles Nelson, '89' of Princeton, New Jersey.

Rensselaer R. Johnson, of Shaker Heights, Ohio, was elected president of the Cleveland Conference of Bank Auditors and Controllers at their recent annual meeting. Mr. Johnson worked in the accrual department of the Union Trust Company from 1922 to 1933, and since 1934 he has been with the Society for Savings Bank. He and *Mrs. Johnson* (Helen Alvord, '20) have a son who graduated from the Cleveland Heights High School this year.

1919 — Class Correspondent: Mrs. Maude

Lichty Perrin, 312 Goodall Ave., Daytona Beach, Fla.

Men in Service

Capt. Theodore E. Lilly, Lieut. John A. Pierson.

Miss Jean Lewis, x'44, daughter of *Mrs. John W. Lewis* (Helen Cole), of Baltimore, Maryland, now has a defense job. Her engagement was recently announced, and she plans to be married in the fall. Mrs. Lewis' son is a junior in high school.

Miss Marion Mair, besides her regular teaching in the New York State Teacher's College at Oneonta, New York, is teaching a Sunday School class and a class in first aid for the Red Cross. This summer she plans to take a course in cowboy dancing at Colorado Springs and to go on a ten-day horseback trip.

Nelson Krehbiel, who is president of the Moundridge Milling Company in Moundridge, Kansas, is busy with defense orders. His daughter is a sophomore in the school of music at the University of Kansas.

Mrs. Joseph M. Kiss (Helen Reed), of Rocky River, Ohio, and her 14 year old daughter, Caroline, spent February 12 in Oberlin with *Mrs. Thomas J. Farquhar* (Katherine Kilmer). Bill Farquhar will be a senior at Oberlin and Mary Farquhar, a sophomore, this fall. Mrs. Farquhar continues as a case worker for the Cuyahoga County Child Welfare Board in spite of the inconveniences caused by tire rationing.

Palmer Lichty Bevis, son of *Mrs. Frederick W. Perrin* (Maude Lichty), of Daytona Beach, Florida, has won during this first year at Yale prizes in Greek and in Latin. He plans to major in government, specializing in the Russian and Malayan languages. His younger brother, Bill Bevis, is attending the Hotchkiss Preparatory School at Lakeville, Connecticut. Mr. Perrin's son, Freddy, is finishing the first grade.

The 1942 Alumni Fund For War Scholarships

1920 — Class Correspondents: Mr. George R. Bent, Berea College, Berea, Ky.; Mrs. Ethel Becker Ellertson, 119 River St., Madison, Ohio; Mrs. Leontine Wright Jameson, 328 Linden Ave., Winnetka, Ill.

Men in Service

Maj. James S. Childers, Lt. Col. Forrester Raine.

Mrs. Lewis E. Davis (Mildred Harter, Con.), of Bronxville, New York, spent May 10 and 11 in Oberlin as the guest of *Mrs. '15'* and Mrs. William P. Davis (Vesper Wood, '15).

Mrs. J. A. Ellertson (Ethel Becker), of Madison, Ohio, writes that P.T.A., choir, and Red Cross work keep her busy. She adds that *Mrs. Ralph T. Hisey* (Anne Billington, Con.'22) led the Madison College Club Choral Group in a concert on May 4.

The twenty-fourth Annual Exhibition of Work of Cleveland Artists, popularly called the "May Show" included several works by Miss A. Vera Otto, Con. The two paintings by Miss Otto which were purchased on the opening day were "Stately Siendour," a sheath of white gladioli, and "Alpha and Omega," dahlias against autumn leaves. Miss Otto is professionally a musician.

1921 — Class Correspondents: Mrs. Marian Warren Moore, W. Jackson St., R. D. No. 1,

Painesville, Ohio; Mrs. Alice Lockwood Andrews, 2627 Ashton Rd., Cleveland Heights, Ohio; The Reverend Mr. Robert Bartlett, 777 Longmeadow St., Longmeadow, Springfield, Mass.

Men in Service

Capt. Charles W. Lauthers, Lt. Com. A. William Loy, Lt. Harold A. Richey. Mrs. Oscar P. Snyder (Louise McDonald).

The engagement of Miss Helen E. Swanson and Carroll L. Lyman, '07' both of Toledo, Ohio, was recently announced.

On May 3 *The Reverend Mr. Robert Bartlett,* of Longmeadow, Massachusetts, preached in the Plymouth Church in Shaker Heights, Ohio. Mr. and Mrs. Wallace Winslow had spread the word of his coming, and a number of "'21ers" attended church to hear him. The group included: Mr. and Mrs. Wallace Winslow, Mr. and Mrs. Wilson Clark (Helen Gray), Mr. and Mrs. Frank Carl (Corinne Evans), Mr. and Mrs. G. Whitfield Andrews (Alice Lockwood), Mrs. Leland D. Longacre (Naomi Ludwig), Miss Wilma Ludwig, Dr. and Mrs. Louie Myers, Dr. Cora Randall, Mrs. Edward Howard (Claire McMurray, x), and her three boys, Mr. and Mrs. Laurence Raymond (Margaret Sill), Mr. and Mrs. Andrew Keep, Dr., '23' and Mrs. Robert Browning (Lucy Beckett, Con. '24), Mr. and Mrs. Richard Moore (Marian Warren), and Betsy and David Moore. Betsy will be a sophomore at Oberlin in the fall, and David entered Oberlin with the June class. Later in the afternoon the group was entertained at tea at the Winslow home.

Mrs. Edward Howard (Claire McMurray, x), of Cleveland, Ohio, was formally adopted by the class of '97 at Commencement time, as the first child born to a member of the class of '97' Mrs. Howard is the daughter of the late James H. McMurray, '97' and Mrs. Kathryn Romig McMurray, x'97.

The Oberlin Shansi Memorial Association has been informed that *Dr. Raymond T. Moyer* has been listed for repatriation from the Far East.

1922 — Class Correspondents: Mr. R. Jack Herberts, 825 Field Bldg., Chicago, Ill.; Mrs. Helen Thomson Will, 40 E. 211th St., Euclid, Ohio; Mrs. Mary Van Brunt Winslow, 4150 Manitou Way, Madison, Wis.

Men in Service

Mr. Laurence M. Plank.*

1923 — Class Correspondents: Mr. Charles Ainsworth, 1433 25th Ave., Moline, Ill.; Miss Helen Van der Pyl, 211 E. 35th St., New York, N. Y.; Mr. Samuel Wilson, 222 Courtland Ave., Park Ridge, Ill.

Men in Service

Capt. Evan W. Scott, Lt. Clyde E. Steele.

Mrs. F. L. Georgette (Jennie Parr, Con.) has moved from St. Petersburg, Florida, to 356 West Stocker Street, Glendale, California.

Miss Marjorie J. Whitlock has moved from Lakewood, Ohio to Rocky River, Ohio. Her address is now 20723 Beaconsfield Boulevard.

1924 — Class Correspondents: Mrs. Anna Wood Armstrong, 36 N. Gamble St., Shelby,

*Anyone knowing this person's full military address please send it to the Alumni Records Office, Oberlin College.

Ohio; Miss Gertrude Nicklas, 3012 Chadbourne Rd., Shaker Heights, Ohio; Mrs. Eleanor Terry Partridge, 130 Edgewood Drive, Stow, Ohio.

Men in Service

Lt. Com. Robert W. Babione, Lt. Arthur C. Bates, Lt. Wendell W. Townsley.

1925 — *Class Correspondents:* Mrs. Evelyn Moulton Chamberlin, 17641 Larchwood Ave., Cleveland, Ohio; Mrs. Mildred Corfman Crowder, 412 Park Ave., Elyria, Ohio; Mrs. C. Esther Balch Hauser, 41 S. 27th St., Camp Hill, Harrisburg, Pa.

Men in Service

Capt. Oscar E. Hubbard.

Mrs. Robert L. McIlvaine (Marian Fisher) has recently moved from Lake Forest, Illinois, to 368 Jackson Avenue, Glencoe, Illinois.

The Reverend Mr. Victor Obenhaus, of Pleasant Hill, Tennessee, was a member of the panel which discussed "The Church and the Redemption of Civilization" at the annual meeting of the Ohio Conference of Congregational Christian Churches May 14-17 in Cincinnati, Ohio.

Mrs. Orin A. Jensen (Marion Afkhauser, Con.) is head of the piano department at the Springfield Conservatory of Music and is doing a good deal of professional accompanying and concert work. Not long ago she was accompanist to a singer at a meeting of the Congressional Women in Washington, D. C., at which Mrs. Roosevelt was the guest speaker.

The Reverend Mr. Max H. Webster, of Burlington, Vermont, is serving as associate secretary of the Vermont Congregational Conference and advisor of the Vermont Youth Council. He and Mrs. Webster, the former Mary Small of Cleveland, have two sons and a daughter.

Dr. Aznive Neressian is practicing psychiatry and general medicine in Norwood, a suburb of Boston, Massachusetts. Besides maintaining a clinic for the poor in Boston, she serves on the staffs of the Norwood Hospital and the New England Hospital for Women and Children.

Howard D. Shaw is agency assistant with the Continental American Life Insurance Company in Wilmington, Delaware. He writes frequently for *Parents' Magazine* and other publications, and is the president of the Lincoln Club. The Shaws have two sons.

Miss Lois F. TeWinkel is on the faculty of Smith College, and writes that she is busy with defense courses and the many extra demands during the emergency.

1926 — *Class Correspondents:* Mr. Charles L. Burton, 2304 Victoria, Whittier, Calif.; Miss Phyllis Osborn, 3621 Locust, Kansas City, Mo.; Mrs. Helen TeWinkel Tyler, 216 Gibson St., Canandaigua, N. Y.

Men in Service

Pvt. Edward F. Crafts, Lt. Carl J. Miller.

Mr. and Mrs. Charles E. Whitney (Laura Schwahn, Con. x'25) have recently moved from Chicago, Illinois, to Crete, Illinois, where their address now is 551 Dunbar Terrace, Lincolnshire.

Mr. and Mrs. Oak D. Wood (Madelaine Swetland) announce the birth of their second child, William, on April 17, in Honolulu. Their daughter, Mary, celebrated her first birthday in April.

1927 — *Class Correspondents:* Mrs. Anne Oelschlager Johnson, 2465 Manchester Dr.,

Ottawa Hills, Toledo, Ohio; Mrs. Harriette Sheldon Rugh, 110 Morningside Dr., New York, N. Y.; Mrs. Dorotha Young Williams, 1492 Roxbury Rd., Columbus, Ohio.

Men in Service

Lt. Robert R. Crawford, Lt. Alfred Jackson, Capt. Paul L. Jones, Lt. John P. Knight, Dr. Edwin O. Niver, Lt. Wayne J. deVyver.

Dr. David L. Dial, for the last five years head of the neuro-pathology department at the State Hospital in Concord, Ohio, died suddenly on April 20. After leaving Oberlin, Dr. Dial graduated from the Western Reserve University Medical School and spent his internship at St. Vincent Charity Hospital. He is survived by his wife, Mrs. Joyce Dial, his mother, Mrs. Clara Partridge Dial, '88' one sister, Mrs. Dwight S. Spreng (Elizabeth Dial, '18), all of Cleveland, and three brothers, Dr. Robert J.'20, and Dr. Ralph S., of Cleveland, and Dr. Donald E., of New York City. He was the nephew of Mrs. Louis E. Lord (Frances Partridge, '99), of Oberlin.

Mrs. A. W. Patterson (Alice Laffer) has moved to Los Angeles recently, and her address there is 4502 Willowbrook.

Alfred Jackson, nephew of Miss Alice Little, '88' stopped in Oberlin recently on his way east

Alumni Association Will Forward Letters

If you wish to address a letter to any Oberlin man in service and you do not have his address, send it in care of the Oberlin Alumni Association. The letter will be forwarded at once unopened. At the same time the offer is good for anyone not in the service. If you are not certain of any Oberlinite's address, send those letters in care of the Alumni Association to be forwarded. In order to make this service function smoothly, it is necessary to keep the Alumni Records Office posted on changes of address. If you have moved recently send a postcard today giving full particulars on your new work.

to report for duty in the army. He has been doing research work for the Standard Oil Company, and has been in the chemical warfare reserve for some time.

Miss Lael Henderson has left Chicago, Illinois, and taken a position with the Women's Guild of the Evangelical Reformed Church of Cleveland, Ohio. Her address there is 2969 West 25th Street.

Mrs. Carrol Aldrich (Alice Coutts), of Derby Line, Vermont, is the immediate past president of the Eastern Division of the American Association of Health, Physical Education, and Recreation, and attended the recent meeting of the Association in Pittsburgh, Pennsylvania.

1928 — *Class Correspondents:* Mrs. Alice

Smith Glenn, 1122 Poplar, Waukegan, Ill.; Mrs. Virginia Tuxhill Kyle, Jr., 247 E. 49th St., New York, N. Y.; Mrs. Elizabeth West Kelly, 4818 N. Kildare Ave., Chicago, Ill.

Men in Service

Capt. John E. Dougherty, Mr. John G. Fleming,* Mr. Nicholas R. Gardinier, Mr. Robert J. Hansel,* Mr. Keith Horn,* Sgt. John E. Rodgers, Mr. Hans Schmidt,* Lt. Com. Guy H. Williams, Jr.

Mrs. Carroll K. Shaw (Conna Bell) and her two children, Betsy Ann and Conna Bell, have left Oberlin to join Dr. Shaw, who has been in Washington, D. C. since January 1. Their address is now 4614 Beechwood Road, College Park, Maryland.

Harold C. Morris, who is now a coach at Wakeman, Ohio, High School, will be head basketball and track and assistant football coach at Berea, Ohio, High School, in the fall. Mr. Morris coached at Maple Heights, Ohio, from 1928 to 1939 and at Euclid Shore, Ohio, in 1940.

George L. Partridge is teaching at Suffield Academy in Connecticut.

Dr. J. Periam Danton, librarian of Temple University, Philadelphia, has been granted a leave of absence, effective June 15, in order to accept an invitation from the Graduate Library School of the University of Chicago to join its staff for the 1942 summer quarter. He will teach courses in college and university library administration. Dr. Danton was recently named chairman of a Research Fund Committee which gives financial aid to faculty members in continuing research in their particular fields, at Temple University.

1929 — *Class Correspondents:* Miss Evelyn V. Latham, 91 S. Cedar, Oberlin, Ohio; Mrs. M. Lois Hauschildt Raymond, 415 N. Jefferson Ave., Dixon, Ill.; Mrs. Ruth Place Rogers, 1601 18th Ave., S., Nashville, Tenn.

Men in Service

Lt. Stewart L. Cushman, Capt. Lloyd P. Hopwood, Lt. Owen T. Jones, Lt. G. Townsend Lodge, Pvt. John A. McCorkle, Dr. Harold F. Wherley.

Mrs. Milton Engstrom (Virginia Kane) is living at 3336 Church Street, Evanston, Illinois, and has a 14 months old son, James Kane Engstrom. She and Mr. Engstrom, who has recently gone into business for himself as a funeral director, have just returned from a vacation trip to New Orleans and Florida.

Mrs. Ray Christensen (Lillah Studley) writes, "In spite of what you are reading in your papers, Los Angeles is still a grand place to live. I am happily absorbed with my home, garden, church, and a night school class in music."

Mrs. Fred Doremus (Alice McCune) writes from Girard, Pennsylvania, that she has a daughter, Sara Elizabeth, born on February 22.

Mrs. William H. Carmichael (Margaret Bane), who used to live in Santa Barbara, California, now lives at 11 Utah Way, Basic Magnesium Town Site, Las Vegas, Nevada.

Mrs. Harvey Bingham (Ruth Williams) reports that she is living at 3325 Lansmere Road, Shaker Heights, Ohio, and that she has a son, 10, and a daughter, three. Her family has quite recovered from a couple of auto accidents.

Dr. Walter S. Phillips writes, "The editor (A. Laurence Muir) and business manager of the

*Anyone knowing this person's full military address please send it to the Alumni Records Office, Oberlin College.

1929 Hi-O-Hi are now in business together here at the University of Arizona. He runs one side of the campus while I take care of the other. Been out here at Arizona in the botany department since September, 1940, when I transferred here from the University of Miami, where I had been for five years. Like my work here where I am in the teaching game only part time, the rest being in research with the U.S.D.A. Family relations: one dog, seven mice, 11 goldfish, and oh yes, I almost forgot—a wife."

Mrs. W. A. Dunbar (Carolyn Drennan) on April 25 moved to a new address in Larchmont, New York. She now lives at 46 Maple Hill Drive.

1930 — Class Correspondents: Mrs. Magda Von Wenck Biel, 18 Woodroff Ct., Oxford, Ohio; Mrs. Annette Church Evans, 477 Davey Ave., Mansfield, Ohio; Mrs. Bonnie Day Griswold, 2482 Kingston Rd., Cleveland Hts. Ohio.

Men in Service

Pvt. Carl Allensworth, Jr., Lt. Anson J. Argue, Lt. Francis C. Oakley.*

Dr. Elton S. Cook left Palm Beach, Florida, on May 12, and his address at present is 6503 Park Lane, Mariemont, Cincinnati, Ohio.

Miss Magrieta Livingston is working with the censorship office in Honolulu, Hawaii.

Jack Adams reports the birth of his first child, Charles Farnham, on January 8. On April 15 the Adams left their home of the past five years in Mount Vernon, Washington, and now live at 141 Cottage Street, New Haven, Connecticut. Mr. Adams will be located at the main office of Associated Seed Growers, Incorporated.

Al Watkins writes from Wallace Ranger Station, Winslow, Arizona, that he has been district forest ranger in the Sitgreaves National Forest since March 1, 1941, and is located 40 miles from the post office and 12 miles from his nearest neighbor. He reports that he had only 47 fires last year, in the wettest season in years, and that at Christmas time he was snowbound for three weeks.

Mrs. Emmet Brown (Lina Yeager) writes from 31 Devon Avenue, Uniontown, Pennsylvania, "At present I'm trying to eliminate the winter's dirt and taking defense classes—first aid and engineering drafting—from Penn State. Sort of 'off the beam' from music teaching, isn't it?"

Mrs. William Paul C. Loane (Florence Parker, Con.) left Ogontz Junior College in May, 1941, and was married in August. After a honeymoon on the Cape and in the eastern states, the Loanes returned to Drexel Hill, Pennsylvania, where Mr. Loane is rector of the Church of the Incarnation. They spend some time playing organ and piano together.

Miss Arlean Weidner, Con., is teaching music in one of the Reading, Pennsylvania, junior high schools, playing organ, directing a church choir, doing a small amount of private teaching, studying piano with a Philadelphia teacher, and reading a great deal. Her new address is 101 Windsor Street, Reading, Pennsylvania.

The Reverend Mr. Robert Burtt reports being very busy in the years since his graduation from Oberlin. In 1933 he received his B.D. from Union Theological Seminary. In 1934 he received the degree of Bachelor of Protestant Theology from the University of Strasbourg, France. From 1934-'37 he was the minister of the Lagonda Avenue Congregational Church in Springfield, Ohio, and in 1937 he became minister of the Mayflower Congregational Church in Detroit, Michigan. In 1941 $60,000 was raised under his leadership for a new

chapel and educational unit, which was dedicated on May 24, 1942. He married Miss Ruth Stanley, a graduate of Hiram College, in 1938.

Harry Serotkin is secretary of the group work division of the Federation of Social Agencies of Pittsburgh and Allegheny County, Pennsylvania. He has a son, David, who is three and a half.

Mrs. Richard Youtz (Adella Mae Clark), of New York City, had a part in the publication of Educational Psychology, a recent book written by four prominent psychologists and printed by MacMillan and Company. Dr. Youtz was asked to read the manuscript and suggest changes before it was published.

1931 — Class Correspondents: Miss Melrose Robinson, 601 E. 9th St., New York, N. Y.; Mrs. Ruth Cross Utley, 1425 E. 133rd St., E. Cleveland, Ohio; Mr. Charles F. Rogers, 123 Jamestown St., Randolph, N. Y.

Men in Service

Corp. Kwegyir Aggrey, Lt. Arthur L. Benton, Mr. Carl Brickley,* Pvt. Harold Hovey, Ens. William N. Ohly, Pvt. Edward S. Peck, Jr.

Hemingway Hines has moved from Wichita Falls, Texas, to 6710 Dickens, Apartment No. 1, in Dallas, Texas, where he is associated with Standard Brands, Incorporated.

Mr., '33' and Mrs. Lionel Lightner (Betty Hill) announce the birth of Lois Anne on May 17. The Lightners have bought a home at 921 12th Street, Wilmette, Illinois.

Mr. and Mrs. Edward L. McCandless (Phillis M. Keeney, Con.), of Buffalo, New York, are the parents of a daughter, Marilyn Sue, born on April 7.

1932 — Class Correspondents: Mrs. Frances Robinson Barthelemy, 1329 Polk St., Hollywood, Fla.; Miss Marjorie Beck, 133 Oak Knoll Dr., Dayton, Ohio; Mrs. Harriet Reid Clapp, Pott Spring Rd., Towson, Md.

Men in Service

Pvt. John H. Barnard, Mr. Everett C. Bracken, Pvt. Arthur R. Burnet, Jr., Corp. Clarence L. Duell, Capt. Philip L. Dunkle, Lt. Elliott V. Grabill, Pvt. Richard F. Kinney, Mr. Robert Largent,* Corp. Charles E. Vogan, Pvt. Robert H. Wilkins, Mr. Joel C. Williams.

Miss Sylvia Hardy.

Mr. and Mrs. S. S. Atkins (Elizabeth Shaffer) have a new address in New York City. They now live at 225 East 74th Street.

John Buchanan, x, of Medina, Ohio, visited former classmates and village friends in Oberlin on Saturday, May 24.

Robert Kilmer has moved from Norwalk, Ohio, and now lives at 3713 River Road, Toledo, Ohio.

Mr. and Mrs. Earl E. Nofsinger (Catherine Brown), of Baldwin Lake, Greenville, Michigan, announce the birth of a daughter, Nancy Kay Nofzinger, on November 16, 1941.

Mr. and Mrs. Cyrus V. Giddings (Elizabeth Hughes, '33) now live at 216 South Scoville Avenue, Oak Park, Illinois. Before May 27 their home was in Piqua, Ohio.

Erwin A. Thomas, Con., received his B.A. degree from Boston University on May 25. His address is now Mission House, Society of St. John the Evangelist, 33 Bowdoin Street, Boston, Massachusetts.

Miss Ruth E. Corbet, M.A., moved on June 1 from Newark, Delaware, to Wilmington, Delaware, where her address is 819 North Adams Street.

Mr. and Mrs. Richard Irwin (Elizabeth James), according to word received by the Shansi Association through the American Red Cross, were located, as of May 1, on the campus of Yenching University at Peking, China.

Miss Marianne Holman, Con., has been teaching public school music for the past eight years in Indiana, and is now the supervisor of public school music in Liberty, Indiana. She still lives in New Salem.

Mrs. Curt Lundquist (May David, Con.) writes that she and Mr. Lundquist left Philadelphia last July, after living there three years. They are now in Winona, Minnesota, where Mr. Lundquist is associated with the Winona Clinic.

Walter Blodgett has been appointed curator of musical arts at the Cleveland Museum of Art, effective Jan 1, 1943, and will give 12 Sunday McMyler organ recitals, starting on October 4 of this year. Mr. Blodgett came to Cleveland in 1931 and for seven years was organist and choirmaster of the Epworth-Euclid Methodist Episcopal Church. He then went to St. James Episcopal Church. Since 1924 he has also served at the First Unitarian Church.

1933 — Class Correspondents: Mrs. Edith Williams Davies, 3081 Huntington Rd., Shaker Hts., Ohio; Mrs. Jean Young Gratz, Bear Ridge Road, Pleasantville, N. Y.; Mr. Frank Percy, Jr., Wagon Hollow, Northfield, Ohio.

Men in Service

Sgt. Harold A. Bezazian, Lt. John L. Doerschuk, Sgt. Albert W. Hardesty, Sgt. Talbot Harding, Pvt. James L. Hastings, Lt. Roland V. Tiede.

Kenneth Storandt is still on the faculty of the New York School of Social Work, Columbia University, and has finished work on his M.S. He is starting his Ph.D. work, but expects to enter the army before long.

Mrs. Charles A. Silvis (Louise Bushyager, Con.) has a daughter, Dorothy Louise, who is now two years old. Mrs. Silvis is helping her husband with selective service medical examinations.

Miss Margaret Ping is finishing her fourth year in Pittsburgh, Pennsylvania. For two years she has been the executive of the Girl Reserve department of the central branch Y.W.C.A.

Mrs. Donald A. Kurz (Pearl Elizabeth Jones, Con.) writes that her address is now 1315 Oak Avenue, Evanston, Illinois. Her husband is a captain in the army, and a quartermaster to the marines in Chicago.

Sgt. Albert Hardesty, of Elyria, Ohio, visited friends in Oberlin on May 11.

Mrs. Howard Flannery (Jane Evans), with her baby daughter, Gale, has come to the United States from Bombay, India, by way of a navy transport. Her husband stayed in India to carry on his firm's business. Mrs. Flannery and Gale are living with her parents in Closter, New Jersey.

Miss Margaret B. McPherson, Con., was married on May 16 to John Wade Dubocq in the James Memorial Chapel of Union Theological Seminary in New York City. The Reverend Dr. Henry Sloane Coffin, president of the seminary, performed the ceremony, and Dr. Clarence Dickinson, organist of the Brick

*Anyone knowing this person's full military address please send it to the Alumni Records Office, Oberlin College.

Presbyterian Church and director of the Seminary's School of Sacred Music, played an organ recital before the ceremony. Mr. Dubocq graduated from Dickinson College, Carlisle, Pennsylvania, in 1940, and on May 19 he received an M.A. degree in Christian Education from Columbia University. Mrs. Dubocq received the degree of master of sacred music from the Seminary's School of Sacred Music on May 19. They will live during the summer in the manse of the First Presbyterian Church, New Rochelle, New York, where Mr. Dubocq has served for the past two years as student assistant to the minister, and will be at the Seminary next year, while he completes his work for the degree of bachelor of divinity.

Mrs. F. Reed Williams (Jane Morrison) now lives at 5904 32nd Street, N. W., Washington, D. C. Before May 22 her home was in Pittsburgh, Pennsylvania.

Miss Ruth Davis, Con., was married on April 4 to Theodore Princehorn. Mrs. Princehorn took graduate work last year at the University of Iowa, and is now teaching music in Owatonna, Minnesota. Mr. Princehorn was a salesman for the Ohio Fuel Gas Company in Oberlin, until he was inducted into the army recently.

Norman B. Miller has a new address in Cleveland. It is 3351 Colwyn Road, Shaker Heights.

1934 — Class Correspondents: Mr. Robert Cornelius, Miami Beach High School, Miami Beach, Fla.; Miss Doris L. Flierl, 276 Highgate Ave., Buffalo, N. Y.; Mrs. Helen Vradenburg Medill, 2242 Glenwood Ave., Toledo, Ohio.

Men in Service

Lt. Frederick S. Albrink, Mr. Carlton Bucher,* Sgt. Robert S. Eisenhauer, A. S. Dean H. Kelsey, Capt. Norman G. Long, Corp. William N. Michell, Jr., Mr. Joseph L. Naef, Lt. Lynn D. Poole.

Mr., T'13, and Mrs. Royal Haigh Fisher (Josephine Wray, '13), of Ventnor, New Jersey, announced the engagement of their daughter, Miss Elizabeth Wray Fisher, to George Wilbur Biro, on February 12. Miss Fisher is the only member of her family who did not attend Oberlin, having graduated from Elmira College in 1939. Her parents, who have recently returned from Yokohama, Japan, are both of the Class of '13' and her brothers are William Fisher, '41' and Henry Fisher, '44.' As of May 6 she was studying at the Cooperative School for Teachers in New York City, specializing in nursery school education. Mr. Biro did graduate work at Columbia University, and later was associated with the New York City Housing Authority. He was recently appointed senior project manager in charge of the Delaware County Trailer Park, a defense housing project consisting of 500 trailer houses to house war workers and their families. It is being operated by the Farm Security Administration of the Department of Agriculture. His temporary address is c-o Taylor, 7 South Chester Road, Chester, Pennsylvania.

Mrs. Thomas B. Locke (Frances Partridge, x) expects to leave soon for Mexico City, where her husband will represent the Goodyear Company. Until recently he has been representing that company in Sumatra.

Miss Everett W. Lemon (Katherine Satterthwaite, Con.) and her husband are both active in the Detroit Alumni group. She has a large class of piano students and has been studying piano for the last five years with Dorothy Duckwitz.

Her hobby is collecting phonograph records and books.

A note from C. Martin Wilbur, '31, gives the following information: "Halsey Wilbur is in Hong Kong, as a civilian prisoner of the Japanese; but so far as his family can learn through his head office, he is well, and not ill treated. He was working in the Hong Kong branch of the National City Bank of New York, and it appears that the Japanese have been using the American staff to assist in closing out the bank, so that Halsey has at least had interesting work to do. No one knows when he may be repatriated."

Russel B. Nye, of East Lansing, Michigan, has been awarded one of the Alfred Knopf literary fellowships of $1200 to complete the biography of John Bancroft.

Armed Forces Need College Men
Give to the War Scholarships

Mr. and Mrs. Richard A. Sheard (Martha B Hopkins) announce the birth of a daughter, Angela Murrell, on April 15, in Cincinnati, Ohio. Angela is the granddaughter of Mr., '08' and Mrs. Russell B. Hopkins (Murrell Edwards, '08), of Cincinnati.

Miss Lois Schoonover is in Washington, D. C., working in connection with the Department of the Interior on "strategic minerals for the Geological Survey."

Samuel C. Newman, M.A. writes that he was married to Ellen Jensen in December, 1934, and that he has been assistant professor of sociology at the University of Louisville since September, 1939. He is serving on various community and university committees in connection with the war work. Mrs. Newman has been employed with the Social Security Board in Washington, D. C. since 1935.

Charles B. Olds, Jr. is with the State Department of Public Welfare in Baltimore, Maryland, as field supervisor in the Child Welfare Bureau. The war increases their responsibilities in such things as planning for evacuation, foster day-care of children of working women, and help to families in case of bombing. Mr. Olds reports the birth of Alice Catherine Olds on March 8, 1942.

Mrs. Robert H. Sager (Geneva Kilgore, Con.), of East Cleveland, Ohio, writes that she has her hands full with the care of Eric, born on October 31, 1938, and Philip, born on March 20, 1941.

Mrs. William G. Wing (Alberta Heiss, Con.), of Pella, Iowa, is teaching piano and organ, besides doing a good deal of war work. She and Mr. Wing, '32' have a new three manual Kimball organ, which she helped plan.

1935 — Class Correspondents: Miss Evelyn Dalzell, 134 Orchard St., Aliquippa, Pa.; Mrs. Adele Coleman Fackler, Box 1111, Southern Pines, N. C.; Miss Elizabeth T. Meyer, 123 Gordon St., Pittsburgh, Pa.

Men in Service

Lt. Francis J. Aerni, Lt. Lawrence L. Beckedorff, Mr. Sidney Davis, Chaplain Charles Fisher, Chaplain Rollin Goodfellow, Mr. Walter S. James, Capt. Louis R. Kent, Mr. Edward W. Pye, Lt. John C. Reid, Mr. Lee S. Riley, Lt. Richard F. Riley, Lt. Robert F. Weber,* Sgt. James D. Wasson, Pfc. John H. Welker, Donald S. White, Petty Officer, Pvt. Robert S. York.

Robert T. Williams' address is now R. D. 5, Binghamton, New York. He has been living on Riverside Drive in Binghamton.

William Partridge, x, is working at the Goodyear plant in Akron, Ohio.

Dr. and Mrs. Bertram G. Nelson (Helen Morrison), of Chicago, Illinois, announce the birth of a daughter on March 23.

Robert M. Burke, of Hamilton, Ohio, was recently appointed assistant superintendent of transportation for Proctor and Gamble, and received his L.L.B. in June. He has a daughter, Katherine Ellen, who was born on June 30, 1941.

The Reverend Mr. Alfred M. Burkhardt, T, is now serving two Methodist churches, one is Windham, Ohio, and one in Braceville, Ohio. His daughter, Carol Elaine, was a year old on April 22.

Mrs. Donald S. Harris (Marjorie Harris) is living in Tacoma, Washington, as her husband, Lieutenant Harris, is a pilot in the air corps and is stationed at Gray Field, Washington.

Philip B. Shuman is teaching in New Milford, Connecticut, at the Canterbury School, a Catholic college preparatory school for boys. He is making application to join the naval reserve.

Mrs. Philip D. Williams (Margaret Titus) is a secretary in a law firm in Columbus, Ohio. Her husband has recently enlisted in the navy and is stationed in Washington, D. C.

Sidney Davis, Con., reports that his work as a member of an air force band is "somewhat different from school music teaching," but that he is enjoying it very much.

Miss Carlotta Hoffman, Con., was married to Walter N. McCutcheon, M.I.T. '34' in 1939, and they now have a daughter, Gail, eight months old. Mr. McCutcheon is superintendent of the White Tar Company of Kearny, New Jersey, but their home is at 36 Comley Place, Bloomfield, New Jersey.

Kenneth S. Cohick, M.A., is working as a seismologist for the Shell Oil Company in Madera, California. His wife is Helen Wilson, of Altoona, Pennsylvania, and they have two children, Sandra, four years, and Christie, six months.

The Reverend Mr. William A. Williams lives at 475 Norwood Avenue, Youngstown, Ohio, and is minister of a Methodist church there. He and Mrs. Williams, Lydia Roehm of Berea, Ohio, have two boys, aged four and a half years and sixteen months.

Miss Ruth M. Brenner is practicing medicine in Manheim, Pennsylvania, where her address is 1335 Main Street.

1936 — Class Correspondents: Miss Lois A. Bingham, Wilson College, Chambersburg, Pa.; Mrs. Edith Bligh Cooper, 2180 Ambleside, Cleveland Hts., Ohio; Miss Mary I. McCullough, Antioch College, Yellow Springs, Ohio.

Men in Service

Sgt. Robert J. Ailey, Ens. James V. Baley, O. C. E. Robert R. Carek, Mr. Gerald Connelly,* Sgt. Burton H. Holmes, Pvt. William K. Huttenlocher, Lt. Robert A. Keller,* Ens. William C. Kidd, Corp. George K. Manlove, Pvt. Uel P. McCullough, Pvt. G. Leonard

---

*Anyone knowing this person's full military address please send it to the Alumni Records Office, Oberlin College.

Padgham, Lt. Carroll A. Peabody, Mr. John J. Portman, Jr.,* Capt. Brooks Ranney, Pvt. Donald H. Williams.

Mr. and Mrs. Henry Boardman (Marjorie Skinner, Con.), of Berwyn, Illinois, announce the birth of Virginia Mae Boardman on May 14.

Joseph T. Avelia has moved from Trenton, New Jersey, to Manville, New Jersey, where he now lives at 75 North First Avenue.

Mr., '37' and Mrs. Robert K. Zuck (Florence McEnally) announce the arrival of a daughter, Julia Margaret, on April 26, in Chicago, Illinois.

James V. Baley received a commission as ensign (ev-g) on May 12, after four months training on the U. S. S. Prairie State, New York City. He rated third in the class of 250 picked college men, and was one of ten to be awarded swords.

Mr. and Mrs. Philip H. Mayer (Margery Moodey) have recently moved from West Berteau Avenue, Chicago, to 3611 North Damen Avenue, in the same city.

Richard Kellenberger is completing work for his Ph.D. in modern languages at Princeton this year.

Myron Nichols is an instructor in the department of physics at Princeton.

1937 — Class Correspondents: Miss Virginia Deringer, 914 S. Crouse Ave., Syracuse, N. Y.; Miss Harriet Irwin, 12510 Mayfield Rd., Cleveland, Ohio; Mrs. Elizabeth Sheiber Lewis, 5607 Pierce St., Omaha, Nebr.

Men in Service

Lt. Douglas D. Beers, Corp. Henry Booker, Mr. Craig W. Borden, Pvt. Sidney D. Bowdler, Lt. William B. Crocker, Sgt. Joseph R. Friedman, Pvt. Charles Fromm, Jr., Pvt. J. Glesner Griffin, A. C. Roger G. Hamilton, Sgt. William H. Hesley, Pvt. Everett L. Holden,* Pvt. William W. Hopwood, The Reverend Andrew L. Johnson, Corp. John R. Kleinschmidt, Lt. Alfred H. Meese, Mr. Edward A. Miller,* Pvt. Laurence D. Perrine, Mid. Ralph F. Portmann, Corp. G. Randall Price, Pvt. Robert E. Quin, Pvt. Joseph J. Reiter, Pvt. Ronald D. Rogers, Mr. David S. Shelton, Pvt. Wilmot C. Sperry, Lt. William D. Tibbetts, O. C. Ben Lee Tufts, Mr. Herbert M. Weinberg, Mr. Fred Wing, Pvt. William R. Winship, Ens. William Harry Wright.

Mrs. Steven R. DeMeter (Lois G. Fees).

Miss Ruth Adena Peal, daughter of Mr., '07' and Mrs. Arthur L. Peal (P. June Durbin, '12), of Upper Montclair, New Jersey, was married on June 12 to LeRoy Philip Graf, '36' of Cleveland. Among the attendants at the wedding, which took place in the Christ Episcopal Church, Cambridge, Massachusetts, were Miss Lois Bingham, '36, of Wilson College, Chambersburg, Pennsylvania, who was maid of honor, and Homer Hartzell, '35' of Cleveland, who was best man. Mrs. Graf received her M.A degree in English from Mills College, Oakland, California, and studied at Teachers College, Columbia University. Mr. Graf took an M.A. degree at Harvard in 1937, and received his doctorate in American history on June 8.

Mr., '38' and Mrs. Leroy E. Peterson (Lois Goodenough) write from South Bend, Indiana, that they have lately seen John H. Cornwall, Jr., '38' John Hull, '38' Charles Coleman, and several other Oberlin men who are attending the V-7 navy course given at Notre Dame.

The engagement of Miss Virginia Deringer to Mr. Arthur T. Thompson, of Hartford, Connecticut, has been announced. Miss Deringer received her M.A. degree in June at Syracuse University, where for the past two years she has been taking the student dean course and has been on the staff of the dean of women. Mr. Thompson is a graduate of Colby College and of Syracuse University, and at present is employed in the actuary department of the Aetna Insurance Company. The wedding will take place early in the fall.

Harry Guenther has a teaching assistantship at Princeton and hopes to complete work on his Ph.D. in chemistry next year.

Before his induction into the army on February 3, Fred Wing worked for more than a year in a New York law office and passed the New York bar exam in June, 1941.

Miss Janice Carkin has completed her third year of teaching physical education at St. Olaf College, Northfield, Minnesota, and is spending the summer with her mother at 25 Aberdeen Street, Rochester, New York. Last summer she and Mrs. Ray L. Ballard (Suzanne Rohn), of Mt. Vernon, Ohio, drove to Montana for a visit of two weeks with a friend at Flathead Lake. She also paid a short visit to Mr. and Mrs. Walter Richards (Jeanne Lesser) and their two children, at Cortland, Ohio.

The 1942 Alumni Fund For War Scholarships

Mr. and Mrs. G. Allen Clark (Martha Eshelman), of Cleveland, Ohio, announce the birth of a daughter, Sara Jane, on March 1.

Miss Margaret Stanion teaches physical education in the grades and high school at Auburn, Indiana. She is planning to spend the summer at the camp in Bevard, North Carolina, where she has spent the past three summers.

Miss Dorothy E. Platt has completed her second year of teaching at Luther Agricultural School in Luther, Michigan. She spent two years doing secretarial work in a Detroit social service office, and now plans to study secretarial courses at Wayne University so that she will be qualified to teach shorthand and typing.

Mr. and Mrs. Robert Boyer (Ruth Boyer, M.A.) have a new address in Elizabeth, New Jersey. They are now living at 224 Mellon Place.

Mr. and Mrs. W. S. Carson, Jr. (Lillis Baker, Con.), of Swanton, Ohio, announce the birth of William Scott, III, on February 9, 1941.

Miss Ruth M. Hendrickson, of Bridgeport, Connecticut, is the co-author of a pamphlet on "Herbs and Their Culture," published by the Connecticut Agricultural Experiment Station in November, 1941.

The engagement of John Francis Rudolph, Jr., son of Mr., '98' and Mrs. J. F. Rudolph of Warren, Ohio, to Miss Elizabeth Jean Darrow, of Hudson, Ohio, was recently announced. Miss Darrow was graduated from the University of Rochester Strong Memorial Hospital, and Mr. Rudolph has completed his fourth year at the Medical School of the University of Rochester.

1938 — Class Correspondents: Mr. David Barry, 5757 University, Chicago, Ill.; Mrs. Phyllis Smith Severance, 353 Harvard St., Cambridge, Mass.; Mrs. Dorothy Hayford Watkins, 712 Portland Way, Pittsburgh, Pa.

Men in Service

Pvt. Frederick C. Anderegg, Mr. Robert A. Anderson, Pvt. Charles W. Avery, Mr. John T. Bucher, Mr. Walter Cooper, Ens. William F. Craig, Ens. Roland P. Durham, Ens. Robert P. Eshelman, Sgt. John V. Finch, Pvt. Gilbert R. Fischer, Lt. Jerome Friedman, Mr. Sumner C. Hayward, Ens. W. Dean Holdeman, Pvt. James H. Hubbell, Mr. John R. Hull, Chaplain Ernest F. Kendle, Ens. Alan R. McGarry, Pvt. Douglas W. Morrill, Corp. James W. Morrill, Lt. Ralph I. Musson, Mr. G. Kenneth Mytinger,* Pvt. Mortimer Nelson, Mr. Paul F. Norton, Sgt. Donald M. Ray, Pvt. J. Vernon Reeder, Pvt. Robert Robson, Ens. Wallace A. Sprague, Sgt. Sanburn Sutherland, Pvt. John A. Wood, Ens. Newell P. Wyman.

Miss Jean Filkins has moved with her family to Inverness, R. F. D. 1, Palatine, Illinois. She still commutes to her job with the telephone company in Chicago.

Miss Eleanor Gish, who has been in Chevy Chase, Maryland, is now living at 5763 Dorchester Avenue, Chicago.

Alfred E. Partridge has finished his first year's teaching at Tulane University, New Orleans, Louisiana.

Miss Catherine C. Agna, Con., was married to Midshipman Edwin W. Barnes, of Richmond, Kentucky, on May 16. Mrs. Barnes has been a member of the music faculty of Eastern State Teachers' College, Richmond, for three years. Mr. Barnes is a graduate of Eastern Kentucky State Teachers' College and received his M.A. degree at George Peabody College, Nashville, Tennessee. Before he entered the navy, he was associated with his father in business.

Mr., '36' and Mrs. Allen M. Bafley (Virginia Patterson, Con.), of Oberlin, announce the birth of a daughter, Linda McNeill, on May 27.

Mrs. Clyde F. Slease (Eleanor Cunningham) is still at Pittsburgh, Pennsylvania, but at a new address—6033 Walnut Street.

Miss Alice E. Mehrling, who has been teaching at Amherst, Ohio, was married in June to Mr. Millard L. Tupps, of Bucyrus, Ohio. Their address is 315 East Charles Street, Bucyrus, Ohio.

Miss Jane Thomas, Con., was married to Mr. William P. Benghauser on December 26, 1941, in Indiana, Pennsylvania. Mr. Benghauser is a graduate of the University of Pittsburgh and is now with the Carnegie-Illinois Steel Company. Mrs. Benghauser is supervisor of music in Reynoldsville, Pennsylvania. The Benghausers expect to make their home in Pittsburgh soon.

Announcement has been made of the engagement of Paul F. Norton to Miss Alison Stuart, of New York City, daughter of the late Professor Stuart of the classics department of Princeton University.

William L. Mezger is now affiliated with radio station WRAL in Raleigh, North Carolina, and expects to enter government service before long. He writes that he occasionally drives to Duke University for pipe organ recitals.

On a recent trip to Washington, D. C., Mrs. Thomas Watkins (Dorothy Hayford), of Pittsburgh, Pennsylvania, enjoyed the hospitality of

*Anyone knowing this person's full military address please send it to the Alumni Records Office, Oberlin College.

Mr. and Mrs. William Smith (Jay Williams, '39). While there she saw Tom Street, Dennis Lindsay, Mr. and Mrs. James Lindsay (Priscilla Shepherd), Elbert Sisson, and Mrs. Albert Sims (Ruth Leiserson, '40). Mr. and Mrs. Smith, Dennis Lindsay, and Elbert Sisson are all in government employ, and Mr. and Mrs. James Lindsay are living in New York City, where Mr. Lindsay is affiliated with a law firm. Mrs. Smith writes that they have recently had a visit from Albert Buchanan, of New York City, and Ensign Robert Hunt, '39.

The engagement of Thomas Street, of Arlington, Virginia, to Miss Judy Hotson has been announced.

Elbert Sisson, of Washington, D. C., was married to Miss Lucile F. Donahue on May 21 at St. Matthew's Cathedral in Washington, D. C.

Miss Barbara Starr was married on April 26 to Dr. Sterling Olmsted in Cambridge, Ohio. Mrs. Olmsted is continuing her work as Y.W.C. A. secretary in Troy, New York, and Dr. Olmsted is an instructor in English at Rensselaer Polytechnic Institute. Their address is 98 First Street, Troy, New York.

Mr. and Mrs. Wendell Hinkey ("Pepper" Taylor, '40) are living in West Windham, New Hampshire, on a farm owned by the Church of All Nations of Lowell, Massachusetts. Besides farming, they are doing social work and religious education.

Perry R. Ayres graduated from the Western Reserve University School of Medicine, in Cleveland, on June 5, and was married shortly afterwards to Miss Helene PurDun.

1939 — Class Correspondents: Mrs. Margaret Komp Brown, 591 Elm St., New Haven, Conn.; Mrs. Marjorie Bender Carlson, 1335 Clayton St., Wilmington, Dela.; Miss Dorothy Eberhart, 3635 Riedham Road, Shaker Hts., Ohio.

Men in Service

Pvt. Donald Balassa, Ens. Bruce L. Bennett, Corp. Fred R. Bentley, Lt. Andrew J. Berger, Pvt. Louis E. Bliss, Pilot Officer Alan E. Bloch, Ens. Thomas L. Boardman,* Pvt. Irvin Bushman, Mr. William Cady,* Mr. R. Thomas Clark, Pfc. Robert D. Cooper, Pvt. Carlyle J. Frarey, Mr. John J. Gerling,* Ens. Robert S. Hunt, CBM Grant F. Kibbel, Corp. Frederick K. Loomis, Mr. John D. Lyman, Jr., Corp. Oliver Margolin, Mr. Ralph M. Mark, Mr. Richard D. Marquardt, A. C. William M. Mettler, Jr., Ym. Sherwood R. Moran, Sgt. C. Bright Munson, Pvt. Sidney Namkin, Lt. Rodney Nudenberg, Cadet Alfred M. Osmer, Pvt. Gilbert W. Porsch, Mr. W. Robert Rich,* Tech. M. James Rogers, Pfc. Robert B. Slater, Cadet Paul M. Surface, Ens. Philip A. Swart, Lt. A. Curtis Tacy, Jr., Lt. Dudley B. Tenney, Mr. Reginald Twiggs.*

Miss Marjory Picker and Robert Kiburtz were married on April 5 and are living in Cincinnati, Ohio. Mr. Kiburtz attended the University of Toledo and the University of Rochester, and is now a dispatch agent for American Airlines. Mrs. Kiburtz has a position as sales representative for Transcontinental and Western Air, Incorporated.

Miss Angelyn Butterfield was married on March 6 to George Leslie Griffith, Jr., in Bethlehem, Pennsylvania. Mrs. Griffith is

teaching girls' swimming and hygiene in the Bethlehem High School. Mr. Griffith is a mining engineer with the Trojan Powder Company of New Jersey.

Miss Catherine Schaefer and Gilbert McEwen were married on March 21 in New Haven, Connecticut. Mrs. McEwen is teaching grade school at Hamden Hall Country Day School. Mr. McEwen, who did his undergraduate work at the University of Iowa and his graduate work at Yale University, is teaching at the Taft School.

Pvt. Irvin Bushman, Con., was the featured baritone soloist at a recent concert at Fort Sill, Oklahoma. He has studied operatic voice for a year at the Curtis Institute of Music, and formerly was a soloist at the Epworth-Euclid Church in Cleveland, Ohio.

Miss Barbara Wriston, of Providence, Rhode Island, received her M.A. degree in history from Brown University Graduate School on May 18.

Mr., '35, and Mrs. Robert Galambos (Jeannette Wright), 32 Irving Street, Cambridge, Massachusetts, announce the birth of a daughter, Joan Bowden, on May 4.

Miss Helena Strassburger, who has been doing graduate work at the Oberlin Conservatory this year, has been admitted to the School of Opera at the Berkshire Music Center for the summer of 1942. She was a guest soloist at the Commencement concert by the combined Glee Clubs. For two years she was in charge of vocal music at the Andrews School in Willoughby, Ohio, and for the past three years she has been director of music at the Plymouth Church in Shaker Heights, Ohio. In 1941 she was winner in the State and District Artist Contest, sponsored by the National Federation of Music Clubs, and this honor entitled her to appear in the national contest in Los Angeles a year ago.

The engagement of Miss Wynona Leete, daughter of Mr. and Mrs. William R. Leete (Anna Kauffman, '15), of Hartford, Connecticut, to Robert Holden Morse was recently announced. Mr. Morse is a graduate of Harvard University, and is now with Pratt-Whitney Aircraft Corporation in Hartford. Miss Leete's father, who was a missionary to China, is now interned in Shanghai.

Private Gilbert W. Porsch was married on April 25 in the rectory of the Cathedral of the Blessed Heart in Baltimore, Maryland, to Miss Lois Anne Glockler, of Erie, Pennsylvania. Mr. and Mrs. Porsch spent a week in New York City after the ceremony.

Miss Margaret Jacobs writes that she is now working for Time, Incorporated, in the advertising department of Fortune Magazine. Her new address is 816 Simpson Street, Evanston, Illinois.

Mr. and Mrs. William F. Deal (Frances Morrison) are now living at 119 North Essex Avenue, Narberth, Pennsylvania. Mr. Deal is the assistant manager of Stouffer's Broad Street store in Philadelphia.

Miss Elizabeth Hufford has been teaching English at Hanover College, in Hanover, Indiana. At Christmas time she spent a week at Cornell University visiting Mr. and Mrs. Edgar Curtis (Betsy McGee), Mr. and Mrs. Charles Nixon ("Pog" McCord), and Mr., '38, and Mrs. Russell Fessenden (Kay Andrus).

Thomas Clark graduated from the Harvard Law School on June 11, and since May 7 has been in training at Squantum, Massachusetts, to become a naval pilot.

Mr. and Mrs. George H. Williams (Marjorie Derr) announce the birth of a daughter, Portia, in Berkeley, California, on May 8.

1940—Class Correspondents: Mrs. Antoinette Zanolli DiBiasio, 217 W. Washington St., Napoleon, Ohio; Mrs. Janice Rudd Greenwood, 1415 W. 101st St., Cleveland, Ohio; Mrs. Marjorie Meermans Twiggs, 10507 Lake Ave., N. W., Cleveland, Ohio.

Men in Service

Sgt. O. Edward Anderson, Jr., Pvt. Robert R. Bell, Pvt. David A. Blodgett, Mr. William J. Castelli, Lt. Benjamin C. Chapla, Pfc. Gerald E. Cole, Mr. Raymond W. Cummings, Lt. Stephen M. Davis, Corp. David C. DeCou, Mr. Philip F. DeShong, Lt. Frederick W. Fairfield, Pvt. Vinton E. Finzer, Pvt. I. Arthur Frankel, Pvt. Frederick E. Frazier, Sgt. Roger H. Garrison, Pvt. Robert M. Grant, Corp. George A. Gray, P. O. Robert M. Grove, Pvt. Frederick J. Herschleb, Mr. Richard L. Hirshberg, A. C. John B. Johnson, Jr., Pvt. Walter C. Johnson, Jr., Sgt. Jack E. Klein, Corp. Ralph M. Knapp, Pvt. Daniel A. Kyser, Corp. Robert A. Lamberti, Pvt. Benjamin C. Litscher, Pvt. Lendrum A. MacEachron, Corp. Frederick G. Marks, A. C. J. Kirkwood Martin, Pvt. Ernest G. McClain, Mr. Raymond L. McConlogue, A. C. Richard McCoy, Pvt. Ian P. McGreal, Pvt. Thomas V. Mistretta, Sgt. Charles F. Myers, Lt. Frederick C. Nichols, Mr. James W. Olsen, Sgt. Charles H. Price, Jr., Ens. Warren G.

*Anyone knowing this person's full military address please send it to the Alumni Records Office, Oberlin College.

Refbord,* Ens. Nelson F. Richards, Lt. F. Rudolph Schmidt, Ens. John D. Simmons, Pvt. Howard M. Stevens, Lt. John Steinbinder,* Lt. Jarvis A. Strong, Ens. J. Raymond Swanbeck, Pfc. S. Lua Syckes, Jr., Mr. Gordon L. Taylor,* Lt. Eugene W. Veverka, Joseph Wagner, Musician.

Mrs. Alan G. Rorick (Evelyn Edwards).

Miss Francis Farnsworth was married on April 5 to John Robert Cameron. Mr. and Mrs. Cameron are living in Ann Arbor, Michigan.

Mr. and Mrs. *Arthur W. Bryan* (Betty Steele) have arrived safely in the United States from Batavia, Java, where Mr. Bryan has been working for the past year and a half. They are now staying in Cleveland.

Harold E. Brailey, Jr. received his M.A. degree this June at Columbia University. He is an assistant in chemistry there and a scholarship holder, and he is now working toward his Ph.D. degree.

Mrs. *E. M. Fleming* (Pat Crew) is doing graduate work in Spanish at Columbia University.

Miss Adne Wayne, of White Plains, New York, was married to *Warren G. Refbord* in the First Baptist Church in White Plains on March 21. Mr. Refbord is now an ensign in the United States Naval Reserve.

Mr., '39 and Mrs. *Joseph Stella* (Edith Cameron), of Kirksville, Missouri, announce the birth of a son, James, in March.

The Reverend Mr. Leroy Cabbage, T, of Homer, Michigan, was elected to serve as moderator for the ensuing year at the spring meeting of Lansing Presbytery, at Holloway, Michigan.

Mr. and Mrs. *Robert Forney* (Elizabeth Marvin) have a six months old son, Michael Marvin. Mr. Forney is teaching instrumental music in Ferndale, Michigan.

Mr. *Howard Latourette* is in medical school at the University of Michigan.

The engagement of Miss *Mildred Zuck* to John Callander Lanphear, of South Euclid, Ohio, has been announced. Miss Zuck teaches at Gates Mills, Ohio.

Miss Eleanor J. Frear has announced her engagement to David Ridge Dugan, of Perry, Ohio. Mr. Dugan is a graduate of Ohio State University.

Richard Achzehner is working for the Chromium Corporation of America in Chicago, Illinois. He writes, "Since I am still in 1A draft class and my residence here in Chicago is temporary and uncertain, I prefer to retain the permanent home address of 31 Summer Hill, Newport, Kentucky, as my mailing address."

John Kirby Bare, of Youngstown, Ohio, received his Sc.M. degree at Brown University Graduate School on May 18.

Mr. and Mrs. *Arthur Eastman* (Becky Miller, '39) are living in New Haven, Connecticut, where Mr. Eastman is enrolled in the Yale Graduate School. Mrs. Eastman has a position in the psychology department at Yale University.

Miss Alice Jones, daughter of Mr., '94 and Mrs. *Eugene E. Jones* of Oberlin, was married on May 28 to Clyde E. Martin. The marriage took place in Bloomington, Indiana, with Dr. W. F. Bohn, '00 of Oberlin, performing the ceremony. During the past year Mrs. Martin has been secretary to Professor Henry R. Hope, chairman of the fine arts department of Indiana University, in Bloomington. Mr. Martin, a graduate of Indiana University, is now employed as research technician to Dr. Alfred Kinsey of the university zoology department. The couple took a short wedding trip through the Great Smoky Mountains, and are now at home at 510 South Woodlawn Avenue, in Bloomington.

Miss Louise Hatch, Con., is supervisor of music in the elementary grades in Bangor, Maine.

Miss Ann Spencer was married to Captain William Law on March 7 in New Orleans, Louisiana, following his return from service in Panama. She is now with her husband at Fort Bragg, North Carolina.

Miss Priscilla Blaisdell was married to Paul B. Blanshard, Jr. on May 30 at Winchester, Massachusetts.

Miss Jean Gleason was married to Lieutenant Mark Pell in Erie, Pennsylvania, on June 9. Mrs. Pell has been an employee of the material catalogue department of the General Electric Company of Erie. Lieutenant Pell received the degree of B.S. in economics at the University of Pennsylvania and is a member of Alpha Sigma Phi fraternity. He has been employed as an accountant at Erie Meter Systems, Incorporated. The couple are at Camp Wheeler, Georgia, where Lieutenant Pell is stationed.

Mr. and Mrs. *Lucien Day* (Lois Scheibe), of Birmingham, Michigan, announce the birth of a daughter, Felicity, on March 31.

1941

Men in Service

Mr. Cyril K. Ainsworth, S. S. J. Plummer Alexander, Sgt. R. Thomas Baldwin, Jr., A. C. Donald L. Bartleman, Pvt. Milton E. Bassett, A. C. Robert L. Beers, A. C. J. Gordon Bennett, Jr., Mr. Philip H. Best, Mr. Paul B. Blanshard, Jr.,* Pvt. Lyman W. Bodman, Pvt. Hugo F. Bouse, Jr., Pvt. Leo Bronsky, Mr. Alexander D. Brooks, Pvt. William C. Burns, Mid. James F. Calvert, Mr. Arthur Cecil,* Pvt. Charles N. Clarke, Pfc. Thomas E. Cramer, Pvt. Joseph R. Creighton, Pvt. John J. DeMott, Jr., Pvt. Alfred L. DiBella, A. C. Harry J. L. Drypolcher, Lt. Thomas C. Dutton, Sgt. William H. Fisher, Ens. Anthony D. S. Florence, Sgt. Irving Foote, Ens. Hilliard Graham, Pfc. George M. Greene, A. C. George T. Grottle, Corp. Robert G. Gunderson, Mr. Frank B. Hanson, Jr.,* Pvt. Robert W. Hart, John W. Harvey, Musician, Pvt. Frank B. Housel, Jr., Pvt. J. Frederick Hughes, Pvt. R. Garrett Ives, Corp. Horace F. Kennedy, Lt. John B. Kidd, Pvt. Frederick Klug, Ens. John F. Kofron, Jr., Ens. William J. Krueck, Mr. William H. Lammers, Pvt. James Leedy, Mr. Raymond L. McConlogue, Mr. Donald E. McGinnis, Mr. Harold M. Messer, Mr. Ray L. Miraldi,* Mr. Garfield R. Morgan, Pvt. Guy M. Raines, Jr., Pvt. Edmund P. Schermerhorn, A. C. Alfred S. Scofield, Lt. Osborne E. Scott,* Mr. Edward M. Shafer,* Cadet John J. Steinbinder, Ens. James A. Sunderman, Pfc. Charles H. Tarr, Mr. Evan S. Tyrrell, Lt. George A. Vradenburg, Jr., Lt. Robert E. Wear, Cand. Martin J. H. Wegman, Mr. Robert M. Wiley, Mr. Harrison A. Williams, Jr., Mr. James R. Wilson,* Lt. Arthur H. Wyman, Mr. Ivan K. Zaharoff.

Miss Pauline Mossman is doing airplane repair work in the sub-depot of the army air base at Salt Lake City, Utah.

Miss Lois A. Koch, of Lakewood, Ohio, has announced her engagement to John Robert Lovett, of Franconia, New Hampshire. Mr. Lovett was graduated from the University of New Hampshire.

Miss Ann Wyatt, x, of Oberlin, was married in Fairchild Chapel on June 4 to *Charles L. Dinkins.* Mr. Dinkins has completed his first year in the Theological Seminary, and he and Mrs. Dinkins are living in an apartment at the Quadrangle.

Ben Clymer is employed as a research engineer by the Ford Instrument Company, in Long Island City, New York. His address is 5 Prospect Place, New York City.

Miss Louise Aiken has recently been awarded two prizes, $50 for a composition for a string quartet and $100 for a song, in the Art Society of Pittsburgh Contest. These compositions, which were performed in Pittsburgh on May 8, were written while Miss Aiken was studying under Professor Normand Lockwood of the Conservatory last year. She is now studying with Mlle. Nadia Boulanger at the Longy School in Cambridge, Massachusetts.

Zeno W. Wicks, Jr. has been awarded a fellowship for work in chemistry at the University of Illinois next year.

Miss Virginia Lyle Cole and *Miss Charlotte Crossley* both received their M.A. degrees on May 17 at the Fletcher School of Law and Diplomacy at Medford, Massachusetts.

Miss Alice Goodier, of Normal, Illinois, and *Willis Yocom,* '40, son of Mr., '09 and Mrs. C. H. Yocom of Oberlin, were married on May 2 in Normal. Dean Thomas W. Graham of Oberlin and The Reverend Mr. Clyde Vance, of Normal, performed the ceremony, and among the ushers were Leonard Dart, '40 and Rogers Spencer, Jr. Mr. Yocom graduated from Massachusetts Institute of Technology in April with a degree in electrical engineering, and he now has a position with the Bell Telephone Laboratory in New York. The couple took a short wedding trip to Chicago, and are now at home at 45 Tieman Place, New York City.

Miss Elizabeth Warner and *H. Edmund Stiles* were married on April 25 at First Church in Oberlin. Their home is at 2787 Avondale Road, Cleveland Heights, Ohio.

Albert C. Beer, of Ithaca, New York, has been awarded the President White Fellowship in physics for next year at the Graduate School of Cornell University. He is now an assistant in the department of physics at Cornell.

The engagement of Miss *Mary Novotny,* of Cleveland, Ohio, to Mr. Lachlan Ferguson Blair, of Cleveland, has been announced. Miss Novotny received a degree in library science from Western Reserve University in June, and Mr. Blair, who studied at Western Reserve, is employed as an architect in the building of defense plants.

Mrs. *Russell Bentley, Jr.* (Grace Van Tuyl) is a secretary at the 26 Broadway branch of the National City Bank of New York, and is living with her parents. Mr. Bentley is at Camp Lee, Virginia.

Miss Barbara King received the degree of master of letters in retailing at the University of Pittsburgh on June 1, and was recently awarded a prize for outstanding ability and scholarship in advertising. She is now working on the executive training squad at Kaufmann's department store in Pittsburgh.

*Anyone knowing this person's full military address please send it to the Alumni Records Office, Oberlin College.

Miss Dorothy M. Swigert, x, of Benton Harbor, Michigan, was recently married to Walter S. Burns, of Pittsburgh, Pennsylvania.

Miss Jane V. Keeler, M.A., was married in Fairchild Chapel on May 30 to Robert W. Dorn, '40. The Reverend Mr. Harold B. Williams performed the ceremony and Professor James H. Hall officiated at the organ. The bride, who received her B.A. degree from Mount Holyoke, has been an instructor in the geology and geography department at Oberlin, and the groom has been a graduate assistant in the chemistry department here. Mr. Dorn has a position with the Shell Development Company as junior research chemist, and after September 1 their home will be in Berkeley, California.

Miss Sarah Ann Clagett and Paul Beaver Arnold, '40' were married on May 29 in the garden of the Clagett summer home, Stormhill, in Empire, Michigan, with Dr. Clarence Ward and Dr. Nicholas Van der Pyl, of Oberlin, performing the ceremony. Allen Siebens, '40 was best man, and among the ushers were James Arnold, '42' Allen Arnold, '44' and Thornton Zanolli, '38' Immediately following a reception the bride and groom left for an extended wedding trip. Mrs. Arnold has been assistant director of recreation at Oberlin this year, and Mr. Arnold, who received his M.A. degree at Oberlin in 1941, is an instructor in the department of fine arts.

1942

Men in Service

Pvt. John S. Aird, Ens. Howard K. Allen, Sfc. John H. Bartow, Pvt. David L. Beaty, F. C. Kenneth Bohrer, Lt. Robert C. Bowman, Lt. John T. Bucher, A. C. Robert W. Chamberlin, Sgt. Robert J. Champion, A. C. Robert S. Clapp, Pvt. C. Jean Cooley, Lt. M. Budd Cox, Mr. Roy Crawley,* Cadet James W. Dessecker, Jr., A. C. Carrol L. Fisher, Pvt. Arthur M. Fowls, Pfc. R. Monroe Harris, Pvt. Charles T. Heater, Mr. Edwin E. R. Heilakka, Cadet Randall E. Larson, A. C. Norman Lyle, Jr., Pvt. Richard P. MacDermott, Ens. Earl S. Mathis, Mr. R. Walker McKellar,* Mr. Harold S. McGinnis, A. C. Harold D. McDowell, Mr. Sydney A. Merrill, Pvt. Charles E. Orbach, Pvt. Edwin D. Parks, A. C. A. Dale Reitz, Pvt. Joseph A. Rogers, Pvt. Randolph H. Smith, Ens. Sheldon D. Smith, Sgt. Alvah C. Turner, Ymn. Ralph H. White, Mr. Peter G. Wilson.*

Miss Audrey Jean Meacham, daughter of Mr. and Mrs. M. R. Meacham (Edythe Ladd, '13), of Baltimore, Maryland, was married to Murrow William Schwinn, '36' on the afternoon of May 26 in the First Church at Oberlin, with Dean E. F. Bosworth officiating. Miss Alice Stratton and Miss Elizabeth Merry were among the attendants, and the ushers were John Faulkner and Winston Day, '43' Mr. Schwinn received his M.A. degree at Oberlin in 1941, and now has a position in the ordnance laboratory at the Navy Yard in Washington, D. C. After a brief wedding trip, Mr. and Mrs. Schwinn are now making their home in Washington.

Mr. and Mrs. Gilbert Kilpack, M.A., of Oberlin, announce the birth of a daughter, Mary Ruth, on May 27.

1943

Men in Service

Pvt. Milead H. Abraham, Pvt. Thomas

Augustine, Pvt. Russell Buck, Mr. Ward F. Chick, Howard D. Crosier, Musician, Lt. Henry R. DuLac, Pvt. Alfred F. Fasola, Pfc. Fred R. Frey, Jr., A. C. Leslie W. Gleason, Jr., Pvt. Arthur D. Goodrich, O. C. Bernard L. Greenberg, Pvt. Jaroslav Holesovsky, A. C. Oscar A. Kenney, Pvt. Herbert M. Krause, Mr. Ernest K. Limpus, Corp. Kenneth L. McAllister, Mr. Hugh F. McCorkle, Sgt. Lew H. Morse, Jr., Mr. Sherwood J. Paulin,* Chaplain Grant Reynolds, Sgt. Harry D. Rhodes, Jr., Mr. John A. Schantz, Corp. Paul M. Sears, Pvt. Ted W. K. Snow, Jr., Mr. John J. Swisshelm, Cadet Robert L. Winder, Pvt. James E. Wood, Jr.

1944

Men in Service

Pvt. Edwin F. Avril, Corp. Walter Babbitt, Pvt. Carl John Busch, Pvt. Herbert H. Deck, Jr., Pvt. John H. Faragher,* Pvt. John W. Fedak, Pvt. Jens V. Hansen, Pvt. Robert E. Huhn, Corp. Philip R. Moore, Pvt. Charles R. Ross, A. C. Joseph L. Whiton, Sgt. John F. Wright, Jr.

1945

Men in Service

F. C. Jack D. Bailiff.

*Anyone knowing this person's full military address please send it to the Alumni Records Office, Oberlin College.

Shortage of Skilled Labor
Slows Physics Building

Work on the Physics building is progressing steadily in spite of handicaps imposed by the war. Were it not for the need for physicists in the war effort construction on the Physics building would have been halted "for the duration" long ago. Under the circumstances it has been allowed to progress though with some handicaps that even government priorities cannot entirely remove. The most serious threat to its continuation is loss of skilled laborers to other projects paying premium wages for overtime, for which there is no provision in the budget for this building. Unless this situation improves, the building will not be ready for occupancy by the beginning of the fall term.

By the middle of June, the outer walls had reached eaves height most of the way around the building. The ground floor was almost completely developed, the first floor partly so, and a good beginning has been made on partitions, piping and wiring for the top floor. The roof probably will go on during July.

Give to the War Scholarships
Through the Alumni Fund

We Proudly Present...

OUR NEW

MAPLE HOUSE

We invite you to visit our new Maple House; it is full of color and charm and fresh ideas, a friendly house with an air of warmth and hospitality. When you cross the threshold, you'll be delighted with the recaptured spirit of Early American days; the fine reproductions of museum furniture, the quaint hooked rugs, ruffled curtains and characteristic wallpapers. Some of the furniture is cherry in an "Old Mansion" finish that blends beautifully with the maple pieces and with the colorful decoration.

You'll find inspiring ideas for town or country houses in these newly furnished rooms; make yourself at home in the Maple House—come soon and often. The Maple House is located on the Fourth Floor Gallery.

The STERLING *&* WELCH *Co.*

1225 Euclid Ave.   PRospect 7000

y Present...

OUR NEW

PLE HOUSE

to visit our new Maple House; it is full of color and charm
s, a friendly house with an air of warmth and hospitality.
ss the threshold, you'll be delighted with the recaptured
American days; the fine reproductions of museum furni-
nt hooked rugs, ruffled curtains and characteristic wall-
of the furniture is cherry in an "Old Mansion" finish that
ully with the maple pieces and with the colorful decora-

piring ideas for town or country houses in these newly
is; make yourself at home in the Maple House—come
The Maple House is located on the Fourth Floor Gallery.

DING & WELCH Co.

PRospect 7000

CPSIA information can be obtained
at www.ICGtesting.com
Printed in the USA
BVHW091237261118
534010BV00012B/305/P